Worms in my Tea

And Other Mixed Blessings

Becky Freeman & Ruthie Arnold

Worms in my Tea
And Other Mixed Blessings

BROADMAN
& HOLMAN
PUBLISHERS

Nashville, Tennessee

Copyright © 1994
Broadman & Holman Publishers
All rights reserved

4261-43
0-8054-6143-4

Dewey Decimal Classification: 248.843
Subject Heading: WOMEN // CHRISTIAN LIFE
Library of Congress Card Catalog Number: 93-37622
Printed in the United States of America

∾

Unless otherwise stated,
all Scripture quotations are from the Holy Bible, *New International Version,* copyright © 1978 New York International Bible Society. Scripture quotations marked (NASB) are from the *New American Standard Bible,* © The Lockman Foundation, 1960, 1962, 1963, 1968, 1971, 1972, 1973, 1975, 1977; and Scriptures marked (KJV) are from the *King James Version* of the Bible.

∾

Library of Congress Cataloging-in-Publication Data
Freeman, Becky, 1959-
    Worms in my tea: and other mixed blessings / Becky Freeman,
Ruthie Arnold.
        p.   cm.
    ISBN 0-8054-6143-4
    1. Freeman, Becky, 1959-.   2. Mothers—Texas—Biography.
3. Mother and child—Texas—Anecdotes.   4.Family—Texas—
Anecdotes.   5. Family—Texas—Religious life.   I. Ruthie Arnold, 1936-.
HQ759.F744   1994
306.87—dc20   93-37622
                                                            CIP

*Dedicated with love
to our children and grandchildren:
Zachary
Ezekiel
Rachel Praise
and Gabriel*

If you would like to have Becky Freeman speak at your event, please call interAct Speaker's Bureau at 1-800-370-9932.

Contents

Acknowledgments

First, we must thank the incredible men in our lives: Scott, Becky's husband, and George, Ruthie's husband, who were our first and most enthusiastic cheerleaders in the project. They allowed us to sit about nine inches from their faces while they read portions of the manuscript, allowing us to observe every twitch, every raised eyebrow, and every grin as they read, knowing we wouldn't be able to stand it long before blurting out questions.

"What? What part? What part did you think was funny? *How* funny? Too funny, or just right funny?"

Good, patient men.

Without Zach, Ezekiel, Rachel Praise, and Gabriel, this book would not have been written. So thank you, children and grandchildren, for the great material.

Other family members gave us the applause we needed while we dwelled in "unpublished purgatory." Beverly Freeman, Scott's mother, penned our first rave review on flowered stationery. Scott and Rachel St. John-Gilbert, Ann Bietendorf, and Jamie Patterson—all know how to gush when you need them.

We owe a particular debt of gratitude to Etta Lynch, Ruthie's sister and Becky's aunt, who is the first professional writer in the family and who gave us invaluable pointers and suggestions.

Mary Rusch contributed a lot to the book, not only in terms of material, but as a continuing inspiration. "Becky," she observed one day, "you *have* to find time to write a book, even if you *do* have the dirtiest floor in America." True words of encouragement.

We feel a sense of gratitude to people in the publishing world who gave us just enough encouragement to keep us plugging along. Mr. Bill Wallace, award-winning children's author, critiqued the earliest manuscript and sent his remarks: "I think it will go. I won't tell you not to be discouraged while you wait, because you will be."

Also to Larry Hampton, a seasoned editor who gave us a great boost when he liked our book, as did Ken Petersen. Ed Wichern, man of God, retired writer, beloved Sunday School teacher, who, along with his wife, Betty Lou, put up with numerous phone calls for advice, each time encouraging us to keep writing and leave the results in God's hands.

Lisa Spaight, Lou Wayne McQuirk, and Jim Wilde may not think of themselves as answers to prayer, but their help with typing, cranky computers, and print outs came just in the nick of time.

And finally, thanks so very much to Vicki Crumpton and the people at Broadman & Holman Publishers who believed in *Worms in My Tea* and felt the time had come to serve it up to the public, so to speak.

We were truly blessed.

∾

Worms in My Tea

Some mothers use TV as a babysitter. Not Becky Freeman. No sir. The first thing every morning, I run outside our lake-side home, look for any small creature that breathes and moves, pop it in an empty butter tub, poke holes in it (the butter tub, not the critter), and my three-year-old, Gabriel, is set for the day.

There have been days, however, when I probably should have fallen back on the TV. One such day began as I sat folding the morning's wash. I noticed with a sense of unease a strange bulge in the pocket of a pair of Gabe's jeans. Gingerly, I forced myself to explore the warm, dark interior of the pocket, reminded of the feeling I had had years before when the bigger neighborhood kids would blindfold us little kids and force us to stick our hands into a bowl of cooked spaghetti, all the while assuring us the bowl contained either brains or guts. I realized, as I explored the pocket under discussion, that I hadn't matured all that much.

My hand enclosed an object that could have been a piece of bark. Feeling false reassurance, I extracted the mysterious bulge.

Can anyone know how black and shriveled and—well, bark-like a frog can be unless they have seen one washed, rinsed, and fluff-dried?

This event set the tone for the morning. Later that same day I turned from loading the dishwasher in time to see Gabe holding a baby turtle by the tail with one hand, scissors poised in the other.

"Whoa, Gabe!" I managed. "What do you think you're doing?" His reply had a "Why do you ask?" tone to it.

"This turtle needs me to cut his ponytail."

That turtle owes me one.

Toward evening that same day, things quieted down entirely too long. (Have you ever wondered why six minutes of peace and quiet feed the soul of a toddler's mother while seven fill it with terror?) On the seventh minute I dropped my chopping knife with a clatter and ran out to the back porch to check on Gabriel. All was strangely calm. In fact, he seemed to be meditating, his gaze fixed upon a styrofoam ice chest waiting to be stored away. Our eyes met when I heard a thumping sound issuing from the closed ice chest.

"There's a cat in there," Gabe said matter-of-factly, jerking his thumb toward the chest. I was not unduly alarmed for the safety of the cat at this point, since I could see the lid of the chest rise and fall with the thumps, but I did move to liberate the animal. As I lifted the lid, I realized with shock that Gabe had managed to fill the chest with water before depositing Kitty. I grabbed the saturated feline by its neck and estimated her to be on about her ninth life. I turned horrified eyes on my son. Like George Washington, he did not lie.

"I put her in there," he confessed. But he had a reason. "She was really thirsty."

Time passes, wounds heal (both to cats and to moms), and life goes on. For several days after that, nothing particularly unnerving transpired. Then one evening at church I looked down from my hymnal to discover that Gabriel clutched yet another wilting frog in his warm little hands. For some unknown reason, Gabe chose this moment to ask in a loud whisper, "Something smells! Is it you?"

Needless to say, I, Gabe, and the frog all needed "Amazing Grace" to survive that service.

But Gabe, our baby, is growing and is now big enough to dig for fishin' worms. What *I* wish is that he was big enough to go *fishing* with them, because he so hates to see them go to waste. Believe me, there is no experience that quite compares with downing the last of a big glass of iced tea only to discover a grayish worm squirming among the cubes at the bottom. "Just look," Gabe cooed sweetly as he showed me a sand pail containing a number of worms he had not yet invited to tea. "See how they love each other! They're hugging!"

But Gabe *is* maturing. Just yesterday he confronted me, hands behind his back with the look of love and pride other children have when they bring their mommies a hand picked flower. Beguiled, I extended my hand where he lovingly deposited a snail, complete with slime.

"It's for you," he beamed. "I love you, Mommy!" Then he kissed me straight on the lips.

Take it from a woman who knows. Snails and worms aren't so bad. Really.

How many are your works, O Lord!
In wisdom you made them all;
the earth is full of your creatures.
PSALM 104:24

Motherhood:
A Can of Worms?

Have you had a chance to read *My Little Bear*?" inquired my friend, Mindy, who holds a degree in pre-med.

"No, I haven't," replied I, a card-carrying member of the National Honor Society. "But have you read *My Little Bunny* yet?"

What was happening? Did we go brain dead when our children were born? Our hearts had long since convinced us to forego careers, if possible, in order to "stay at home" (any housewife will chuckle at that expression) with our children, at least until they started school. But then, as I observed my husband Scott studying the best-seller, *Dress for Success*, I also observed myself, dressed in standard, faded purple, Porky-Pig sweats and felt qualified to write my own version: *Dress Like a Mess*.

That was the night I decided to write a book. A real one. I wasn't motivated so much by the desire to make my mark as I was the need to put down on paper for myself—and maybe others—the reasons I believe making a home and building a family is important and worthwhile. I had seen a demonstration of that in the family from which I sprang (sprung?) and I feared such families are getting scarce as hen's teeth.

Beyond that, I wanted an excuse to share the fun of the simple, yet profound, children's chatter that makes up so much of my days with my four little people. I also had in mind that the project might help keep my gray matter from permanent atrophy while I put my college education on hold. I figured it might even keep some other mom from thinking *her* atrophy is permanent or from prematurely throwing in the towel.

If nothing else, I figured I'd have something to read when it's all been said and done and I must pass through the valley of the shadow of the empty nest syndrome, which the experts all agree I must endure if I don't develop a life of my own. Personally, I expect at that time to be busy dancing a jig and going out to dinner every night with a deliciously adult husband, like my own parents are now doing.

It occurred to me that Mother might give me a few pointers. She had pounded the typewriter on and off through my teen years, writing Sunday School curriculum and other things that had gotten into print. It didn't look all that hard, so I broached the subject by phone.

"Mother? I just read the funniest book. I think it's called *Stick a Geranium in Your Hat and Smoke It*. Wanna write a book with me?"

She seemed to hesitate for a moment, and I may have heard her sigh before she answered, "Sure. Why not?"

We decided to begin with the subject of motherhood and branch out from there. There *are* tricks to the trade of mothering and I have a few of my own. In order to see mothering from the most positive perspective possible, rather than as a can of worms,

I invented a mental game to play with myself. I pretend I am Erma Bombeck and write down each disaster as if it could—someday—be funny. So you see, I already had quite a stack of notes for My Book.

Not everything my little people have said and done has been a disaster by any means. On some days I have felt certain that, just as Mary Poppins said of herself, they were "practically perfect in every way." Such was the day I took our third child, three-year-old Rachel, to the bathroom at Burger King. From inside the bathroom stall I heard, "I love you, Mommie. Aren't we *both* so sweet?"

Remembering another occasion with Zeke, our second born, I can still feel his grubby little hands gently caressing mine as he said, ever so kindly, "Your hands are getting a little old, Mommy. But they're not as crumbly as Nonnie's." He was lost for a moment in his dreamy world, but then finished, "I still love *her.*"

And I melt. Perhaps having a glamorous career isn't nearly as gratifying, after all, as being sweet and crumbly.

Whoever loses his life
for my sake will find it.
MATTHEW 10:39
&

Curbin'
Their Wormin' Ways

E verybody knows that children must be disciplined. That is, everyone except the children. What parent has not faced down the toddler who declares through his outthrust bottom lip, "You not the boss of me!" Then ensues a scene not unlike the shoot-out from *High Noon*. Hopefully, Mom (or Dad) is the one left standing.

Now, discipline has never been my strong suit, partly because of my Erma Bombeck vow to try to see the humor in a given situation. I also find it impossible to frown and laugh at the same time. I knew I had a problem with discipline long before the day I discovered my first-born, Zach, age three, engrossed in the contents of my make-up kit. With proper anguish and indignation, I confiscated his supplies and began the scrubdown.

Suddenly, he pointed his chubby finger at me and said in a voice that would have put Isaiah *and* Jeremiah in the shade, "I'm gonna tell God you took that make-up away from me!"

"Well," I responded firmly, "God sees everything and He knows you took my make-up without asking me."

Silence. Then very quietly he admitted, "Oh. I not be frazy bout that."

Ah, discipline. Ain't many of us frazy about it. And kids know all the angles. The important thing, say the experts, is not to let them worm their way out of it.

At age two, reasonableness was not Zach's strong suit. If I failed to cut his peanut butter sandwich into a perfect right triangle, he would throw himself to the floor thrashing, screaming and nearly foaming at the mouth. To handle the situation without getting physical, I was faced with the prospect of hiring a professional draftsman to bring his protractor and Xacto Knife™ and cut the sandwich. The other possibility was to call the folks at the zoo to come with their tranquilizer guns.

Neither alternative seemed really practical, so I faced the showdown, shades of *High Noon*. However, he must have seen the spanking coming because he stopped the tantrum virtually in mid-air. He wrapped his chubby little arms around my knees and lisped, "I wuv you. I give you big kiss."

What's a mother to do? Spit in his eye?

The books tell us the goal of disciplining children is to teach them to become self-disciplining. A few weeks after I had determinedly dealt with Zach's sandwich syndrome, I made the mistake of cutting his sandwich diagonally from top left corner to bottom right rather than vice versa. I was pleased and surprised when instead of throwing his usual tantrum, he said with great restraint, "This is *not* funny, Mother."

Being new to motherhood and partial to any "natural" philosophy of raising children, I bought into the whole Earth Mother ideal. It goes without saying that I was one of those women who breast fed their babies until they were old enough to cut their own meat.

But when I got the literature on "The Family Bed," I felt relieved and reassured, since Zach spent most of his nights in our bed. Little did I dream how crowded our nuptial bed was destined to become. When Zeke made his appearance, I decided one night to try to persuade at least Zachary to sleep in his own big bed, offering an inspired suggestion.

"Zachary, wouldn't you like to snuggle up with this nice big Pooh Bear™?"

He took one look at the teddy bear bait and tearfully sniffled, "I'd rather snuggle up with a nice big mommy."

So, for several years following, the children would file one at a time into our bedroom at night like silent sleepwalkers muttering, "I had a bad dweam," or, "I cold in my woom," knowing I was a patsy for frightened or freezing children.

Scott and I were frequently waking up with a vague feeling of never actually having slept, as we clung tenaciously to the sides of our bed in areas the size of small tea towels. The children, however, remained sprawled in our bed while visions of sugar-plums danced in their heads, so blissful were they. My husband and I, without kerchief or cap, began to dream of a long winter's nap.

Fortunately, I came to realize that a tender-hearted sucker does not always a good mother make, nor any sleep receive, and I began to move from the Back to Nature literature to the Dare to Discipline genre.

Sooner or later, however, comes a day when our children echo back to us the words of discipline we have taught them. One evening some years back before Gabe joined us, and after a late bedtime fiasco on an evening with no relief from a late working, stressed for success daddy, I had come to the end of my patience. I ordered the boys to bed, plunked Rachel on the couch and sentenced her to lie there until I could get a grip on myself. I began furiously loading the dishes into the dishwasher, grumbling to myself all the while until, like a balloon out of air, I exhausted my anger. Rachel, noticing a quieting in the kitchen, bravely peeked over the back of the couch. She smiled knowingly and spoke in a most maternal tone of voice.

"Are you ready to behave now?"

No discipline seems pleasant at the time, but painful.
Later on, however, it produces a harvest of righteousness
and peace for those who have been trained by it.
HEBREWS 12:11

Mother Earth Worms

There are three kinds of people in this world: right brain creative types, left brain organizers, and people who cannot seem to locate cerebral matter in either hemisphere. I am whichever brain it is that can organize her thoughts on paper, be a member of numerous honor societies, and still manage to wear her dress inside out all day without noticing it.

People seem to be born either basically organized or artistically creative, but rarely both. My little sister, Rachel (out of admiration for whom I named my daughter), and I are prime examples of both extremes. When we were children living at home, her belongings were so organized that I could not filch so much as one M&M™ from a mammoth Easter basket without being called to account for it.

I recall a morning when I desperately needed to borrow a clean blouse from her closet because mine were all in use, piled on the carpet in the corner of my room to hide a Kool-Aid™ stain from Mother. I opened Rachel's door ever so quietly and tried to tippy-toe into her room without waking her. She never moved, never opened an eye, but said in what I thought was an unnecessarily threatening voice, "Don't even *think* about it."

Even our choice in clothes reflected our different personalities. As we grew to be teenagers, Rachel opted for a few well-tailored, quality suits. I, on the other hand, had a closet full of bargains with lots of ruffles, lace, and color.

Our courtships and subsequent marriages also revealed our right brain/left brain contrasts. Scott and I fell hopelessly in love at the ripe old age of fifteen while on a mission trip to El Salvador, digging ditches for an orphanage. We married at eighteen, full of happiness and thinking very little about the things money *could* buy—food, clothing, shelter, gasoline...We would simply live on our love, which we were certain was the greatest since Romeo and Juliet.

But my little sister kept her head about her, even in matters of courtship. First, she graduated from college and then, at a respectable age, met her potential lifetime partner, another Scott: Scott St. John-Gilbert, no less. (I like to call him Gilley.) Before rushing into marriage, Rachel and Gilley ran through a series of personality compatibility tests and endured agonizing spiritual searches to determine God's will in the matter. After their tentative budget was planned and their five-, ten-, and fifteen-year goals carefully drawn up, they plunged down the aisle with reckless abandon.

With their Five-year Plan right on track, my penny-wise sister and brother-in-law saved their D.I.N.K. earnings (Double Income, No Kids) to purchase a lovely condo overlooking a golf course. For the time being, I will describe our country home as "rustic." I see no need to draw any further comparisons with regard to housing. Rachel and Gilley soon purchased a houseful of Ethan Allen furniture, in white. When I purchased a new couch, I chose a tan and burgundy print for its ability to blend with peanut butter and grape jelly.

One might expect that in bearing children, we are all sisters under the skin, which is true. However, no two births are ever exactly alike, and Rach and I even bore children under incredibly different circumstances. When Zach was born in the late seventies, the watchword of the young and idealistic was "Back to Nature!" Lamaze was the only way to go. Therefore, I would give birth in the warmth and intimacy of our own home. No conventional doctor, antiseptic hospital or pain blocking drugs for me, no siree.

On a Saturday morning in early December, I began to experience signs that this might be The Day. We notified our male midwife and he promptly appeared at our door, did a quick exam and agreed with our diagnosis. However, he said there was no rush to boil water or tear up a sheet for white rags. It would be a little while yet. He sounded light-hearted and wonderfully reassuring and when we asked about going out to buy a Christmas tree to decorate in order to pass the time, he thought it was a jolly idea.

We notified our folks and before they could throw down the phone and jump in the car we told them it might be as long as six or seven hours. "No rush."

That evening, ten hours later, Mother served barbecue to us and the midwife and his red-haired female assistant. (No need to worry about nausea, since I *definitely* would not be having any anesthetic.) Not much progress had been made other than a nicely decorated Christmas tree, but we were all still smiling and in a companionable mood. The lights of the tree blinked gaily in the deepening twilight. The midwife was dressed in a T-shirt and jeans, and he told us during supper that he was a former Marine sergeant.

After supper, he announced that I needed to get busy walking to speed things up. At 2:00 the next morning, Scott was literally walking me through the house, standing behind me, holding me up and moving my feet with his feet. Mother was chewing her lower lip and glancing at the back bedroom, where sounds of the midwife's snoring issued forth, making her nervous. He was confident we were in good hands with his assistant, but at 3:00 A.M., Mother decisively made her point. We called out the Marine.

We had figured things had to get tougher before they got easier, but when Mr. Midwife speeded things up, none of us were prepared for three hours of pushing. If I declined to push, the ex-Marine barked orders at me in such a way that I discovered there was one more push left in me after all. Scott's mother had dropped by for coffee eighteen hours earlier, and still had enough of her wits about her to photograph the proceedings. My own mother was gyrating between moments of deep prayer on her knees in the kitchen and babbling idiocy.

As for the prospective mother, I would have cheerfully strangled every natural childbirth expert who had ever told me that labor was not painful, just hard work. This was *PAIN*.

Scott supported my head and shoulders and coached, "Just think, the baby's almost here!"

"Just think," I shot back, "if I get out of this alive, you are going to be living a celibate life!"

At 6:30 that morning, twenty-one hours after we had so blithely welcomed the first signs of impending birth, the midwife laid my 9 lb., 2 oz., son in my arms. Maybe the fact that I am five feet two and small boned accounts for Zach's taking his good old time to arrive, but it was suddenly all very worth it. So much so, that we managed to keep having children. And having them. And having them.

The birth of Baby Number Two seemed like a piece of cake in comparison to Baby Number One. Zeke arrived at mid-morning on a rainy June day, assisted into the world by a highly competent midwife and her two assistants. (As an aside, I might mention the Marine had made the front page of our metropolitan newspaper, having been arrested. This is a true story.)

Baby Number Three would have none of making her appearance on a warm summer morning. The holiday season seems to be the first choice birthing season in our family, and Rachel Praise chose to make her debut three days after Christmas in 1983, one of the coldest winters in the history of the United States. Condensation froze on the windows *inside* the house, and snow and sleet fell in heavy sheets outside our tiny home. My parents and my sister, Rachel, eighteen at the time, were visiting for the holidays, and they all needed to return home. I was overdue, and felt like a watched pot waiting to boil. I had already imagined several instances of labor pains about which we had notified our female midwife (a good friend by this time), but so far, I had been unable to produce a grandbaby and a niece/nephew for my audience. But at about two in the morning on December 28, I woke Scott to tell him I was in labor.

"Go back to sleep," he yawned. "I don't even think you're pregnant anymore." The interesting thing is, I managed to do it, but when I next woke up, there was absolutely no doubt. I *was* pregnant, but I wouldn't be for long.

The scene that followed was like a choppy Keystone Cops episode. I yelled orders while Scott scrounged in the closet for the box of supplies I had assembled for use by the midwife. I realized the box was now the "Do-It-Yourself Birth Kit" because the midwife was thirty minutes away in *good* weather. So much for the LaBoyer method I had wanted to try.

Daddy got on the phone to the midwife, relayed messages to Mother, who hollered them to Scott, who was the most qualified at this point to officiate since he had assisted at the first two home births we had hosted. In the meantime, Rachel took careful notes in the section of her looseleaf organizer entitled, "Things I Must Never Do." Then she dived in like a trooper, ready to boil rags or tear up sheets, though we never figured out what we should have needed either for.

When the baby was born into Scott's waiting arms, he tearfully announced it was another boy. A few seconds later, Mother said, "Scott...um...I think you were looking at the umbilical cord there." We named her Rachel Praise, meaning "God's Innocent Lamb of Praise."

The midwife arrived in time to tie the cord, and Scott, now full of pride and self-confidence, allowed as how he might offer a free baby delivery with each new home he built thereafter.

Three years later, Gabe arrived, and the birth happened so swiftly and smoothly that my mother didn't make it in time for the actual event, to her everlasting gratitude. During my recovery, she managed the three older kids and our household just fine, but Gabe was a little hard on her back. He had weighed in at ten pounds plus. Talk about your grand finale.

On the first day of February 1992, my sister, Rachel, gave birth to her first child—her way. She went into labor after a full night's rest at about seven in the morning on her day off. Seven and a half hours later, she called me from the exquisitely beautiful and home-like birthing room at the hospital to tell me in graphic detail of the two painful contractions she had endured before calling for the epidural.

"After that," she reported enthusiastically, "it was great. We all sat around and laughed and played Gin Rummy." That evening when I called to check on her and her new son, she could hardly talk because she was chewing steak from the candlelight dinner the hospital had served her and Scott. She apologized for cutting me short, but she had to call the gym and make her next racquetball appointment before it closed.

Good grief! I mentally ground my teeth. *She has managed a Yuppie childbirth!*

As memories of my totally natural Lamaze, LaBoyer, LaLudicrous births swept over me, all I could think was, *What was I thinking?*

In retrospect, I draw some comfort in wondering if the modern way of giving birth in those beautiful birthing rooms with loved ones about would ever have happened if a generation of Mother Earth devotees had not put their collective foot down. Maybe I had a tiny part in helping to make my sister's childbirth experience one she will always cherish. I hope so.

And as time progresses, I fully expect that my new nephew will sleep through the night throughout his infancy, develop into a child prodigy at the piano, and as a teenager frequently ask, "What else can I do to help you, Mother?"

In reality, however, it is the differences between my sister and me that keep us fascinated with each other's lives. As women, we have grown to admire and love each other more with each passing year, due to a good deal of acceptance and understanding. She has always loved Scott, me, and our children unconditionally with abounding enthusiasm.

So even though Rachel *does* have a twenty-two inch waist (I honestly don't know how she does it), had a quick, painless childbirth, and owns furniture that doesn't stick to the seat of her guests' pants, how could I help loving her?

The body is a unit, though it is made up of many parts;
and though all its parts are many, they form one body.
So it is with Christ.
1 CORINTHIANS 12:12
☙

From Grub Worms to Grandeur

The scene is the Dallas-Fort Worth Airport, Summer 1974. Scott's mother, Bev, and my mother, Ruthie, are standing near the boarding ramp watching their teenage offspring depart for a summer mission experience. As the plane shrinks to the size of a toy in the warm Texas sky, Mother turns to Bev, and sighs deeply.

"I feel better knowing that Becky is with Scott. She needs someone to look after her because she'd lose her head if it weren't attached."

"Mmmm," said Bev.

"Mmmm?" said Mother, registering concern. "Mmmm what?"

"Actually, I was hoping Becky might help Scott keep up with *his* things."

The two mothers grip the guard rail a teensy bit tighter, suddenly realizing their fifteen- and sixteen-year-old children are headed for El Salvador to help construct a church building, and neither can be trusted to keep up with their shoes, let alone their passports.

Meanwhile, up in the air, I was having my own thoughts. They went something like this:

Lord, I'm so excited. Scared, too. I'm glad Scott will be with me on this work team. He's in good shape so he can probably show me how to dig or saw or whatever it is I'm supposed to do. I did do a couple of sit ups this morning. I think I feel stronger already. I checked to be sure no one was watching, flexed my best muscle, then passed some time trying to locate it.

Too bad I'm not going with his big brother instead. I'll just never get over Kent, no matter how hard I pray. It hurts even to think about the moment he broke up with me. And that was ages ago.

Maybe this mission trip will help me focus on You, Lord. I really do want to learn to love You more—and my teammates, and all those little brown skinned children I plan to adopt someday.

Scott tells me his thoughts went something like this: *YES!!! I have Becky Arnold with me for seven weeks! YES! YES! YES!!!*

Scott and I had known each other for several years, getting to be buddies in our youth group. My folks knew his folks from church also, but the church was a big one and they hadn't spent a lot of time together. What I did not know is that Scott had spent several afternoons visiting with my mother, trying to find out what it might take to win some points with me.

"I hated to tell him he needed to grow at least another ten inches taller," she later laughed. As it turned out, he did manage another eight, and, in the space of a few months, zoomed from five feet four to six feet. And I hardly noticed. But, back to the summer of 1974.

Before we could leave for our final destination in El Salvador, we had to go through a type of boot camp somewhere in the swamps of Florida. When we arrived at what appeared to be a refugee tent city, I turned to Scott hopefully. "Where do you suppose is my condo?"

He grinned and squashed a mosquito the size of a small chihuahua feeding hungrily on my arm.

"This is *great!*" he beamed, and I realized with awe that he actually meant it. Soft spoken, mild mannered Scott Freeman transformed before my very eyes into MacGyver and Rambo combined. And I, Miss Teen Femininity, would soon find myself living in denim overalls and army boots. Little did I realize how long it would be before I enjoyed a hot bath or air conditioning again. At the moment, only one of us was a genuinely happy camper.

I soon found my quarters for the next week, a tent filled with girls from as far away as Hawaii and Canada, most of whom looked as bewildered as I. A beautiful Hawaiian girl, Canaca, sped up the female bonding by sharing a forbidden bar of chocolate from the islands with all of us. Strengthened by the sugar and her kindness, I decided to open up real communication.

"Thanks for the candy! Where're all of y'all from?" I drawled. A bouncy blond was the first to respond.

"I'm from New Yoik." Talk about fascinated. To me, she sounded exactly like a cab driver in a movie I'd seen. Apparently she found my accent equally entertaining. She looked at me as if I were an alien from another planet.

"Hey, Tex, is that accent for *real?*" she squealed.

Before I could drawl "Yep" to the miniature "New Yoikuh," the dinner bell rang, and we trudged to the soup line arm in arm.

I was famished. But as soon as the server handed me my tin bowl of chili, I tripped over my new boots and deposited most of my one course dinner on a fellow teammate's back. I did the best I could to scrape the beans off his shoulder with my spoon.

"I guess that's why they call it the mess hall," I offered, but he didn't see the humor of the situation. Looking around to see who had observed my graceful dive, I saw Scott grinning at me from his seat in the corner of the makeshift dining hall. I blushed clear down to my steel-tipped toes.

I had lived to the ripe old age of fifteen, and accidents like spilling chili down a stranger's neck were already fairly common. I usually took them in stride, but this time was different. A whole new set of thoughts tripped into my dithered head.

Scott looks so tall. Has he always been so handsome?

He stood up slowly, stretched to his full six feet, glided toward me with the litheness of a cat—and slammed face-first into a tent pole.

Oh, my goodness! my heart beat wildly. *He's perfect!*

After dinner I wandered exhausted through the sea of green tents, trying to remember which one was home. Eventually I found my pillow and, after saturating myself with insect repellent, I fell soundly asleep. Minutes later, or so it seemed, I heard a voice in the dark outside the tent.

"Time for calisthenics! Up and at 'em!" I recognized Scott's voice as he bounded by our tent. Any romantic thoughts I had entertained the evening before evaporated. The only difference between me and a rattlesnake in the morning is that I bite with less provocation.

"Just let me at him!" I growled to myself. "I'd like to personally give that boy a root canal—minus anesthetic."

I yanked my overalls on, inside out and backwards, and managed to crawl out the tent opening. I squinted toward the red ball peeping over a palm tree in the east.

So that's where the sun comes from, I thought groggily.

Scott was merciless, leading our team in a workout that left me feeling like a wad of silly putty. Too late I remembered he had taken gymnastics for years, which may have accounted for the Adonis build. Even in the dim light of dawn, I had to admire his tan, his perfect white teeth, the straight golden brown hair falling over his brown eyes, the square chin…At the moment, however, the girls in my tent desperately wished I had brought along a fat Texas couch potato named Bubba instead.

That was on Monday. By Friday, Scott had whipped us into shape and the physical obstacle courses had united our rag-tag group into a real team. During the day we learned to tie steel, mix concrete, and lay brick under a blazing sun. In the evening, camp meetings inside the big tent under the stars were precious times of worship and refreshment. There was one night in particular I will never forget.

It began after an especially moving devotional. I was kneeling at the front in prayer when I glanced behind me and saw Scott kneeling at the altar, too. I looked into his face, and he into mine, and it seemed as if the dirt floor became holy ground. Like some ethereal dream, everything around us stopped and quieted and blurred, except for what was clearly happening between the two of us. A strange thought shot through my mind. *This young man will be your husband someday.*

Then Scott reached for my hand and held it for a few seconds, our eyes unwavering.

"I love you, Becky," he whispered. "I always have."

"I love you, too." My lips formed the words before my mind could talk my heart out of it. Could it be that I was falling in love with a friend? A buddy? *Kent's little brother?*

As I walked back to my tent in a world that had changed forever, I found myself thinking with wonder, *Little brother has grown up.*

I was shaking when I slipped into my sleeping bag, and to calm myself I reached for my Bible under my pillow. I fumbled for my flashlight and opened to Jeremiah 24:6-7: "My eyes will watch over them for their good…and I will build them up and not tear them down; I will plant them and not uproot them. I will give them a heart to know me, that I am the Lord. They will be my people, and I will be their God, for they will return to me with all their heart."

Somehow I knew that those verses were especially for me and Scott that night and that good things lay in store for us in the days ahead, perhaps even in the years ahead. Now one might say, "We are talking about a fifteen-year-old girl and a sixteen-year-old boy here!" And I would agree. Serious relationships almost never begin, and even more rarely last, at those ridiculous ages. But sometimes, miracles do happen.

The week in boot camp passed and the day finally arrived when we were to leave the Florida swamplands for the country of El Salvador. The plane flew over emerald-green hills decorated with beautiful patchwork fields, then passed over Lake Illapango shimmering in the sunlight. Once on the ground, I fell in love with the people immediately. I couldn't understand a word they were saying, but I did my best.

"¡Bienvenidos!" greeted the dark-haired hombre who met our plane.

"Sí," I responded politely. "Picante salsa chili con enchilada," I said, quite pleased with my perfect Spanish accent. The man looked impressed and was wonderfully warm and welcoming. I still cherish the warm feelings of affection in my heart for the hospitable people of Central America.

Our team of about thirty teenagers and three married couples found our accommodations to be much more luxurious than at boot camp. We girls were housed in a chicken shack, a great improvement over tent city, and I think the boys got the goat barn. Our mission? Prepare a huge foundation for a Christian camp for native children, without the aid of any modern equipment. I developed a new empathy for the children of Israel in Egypt, building pyramids for the Pharoah after first building their own bricks.

Because we had had to pack so sparingly, the toughest part of the summer for me was spending almost every day in my huge, smelly overalls. Our days started at 5:30 A.M. and were filled with mixing concrete by hand, digging endless chunks of dirt from the sides of a mountain, wheelbarrowing, and tamping, which meant pounding dirt for the foundation with cans of cement attached to a broom handle. I must confess, I perspired. Actually, I sweated. In fact, I could hardly stand the smell of myself. I thanked God everyday that our chicken shack home had no mirror so I did not have to see my own reflection during those weeks.

Most of the time I was a trooper. When a rat ran across our beds one night, I did not keep screaming on and on and on like some of the girls. Although I had to get up before the sun and had been on ditch-digging duty from dawn to dark, I did not complain. But I *hated* those overalls. They made me cry. Every day. In a way only a fifteen-year-old girl can. Daily, I washed them with bar soap like the native women. I poured an entire bottle of perfume over them. Still, they smelled like rotten eggs and made me look like a hayseed.

One morning during devotions, I caught a whiff of myself and my overalls, and off I went into a crying spell again. I felt sorry for myself a good long time, and then I reached for comfort again. The Lord reached back to me this time through the book of Job: "Even if I washed myself with soap and my hands with washing soda, you would plunge me into a slime pit so that even my clothes would detest me" (9:30-31).

Job and I had become soul brothers in whining, and it was then, at a young and tender age, I realized God must have a sense of humor. I wiped my tears and grinned. After that, the overalls were a little easier to bear.

On Saturdays, we enjoyed glorious freedom, except that boys and girls were not to pair off. Our chaperones allowed us to roam the markets and villages by ourselves, once we had walked the five miles to town. I think they figured we'd be too exhausted to stir up much trouble after a long hike in the El Salvadoran sun.

I immediately bought a beautiful, floor-length, turquoise-colored dress, richly embroidered with red roses and deep-green leaves. I was already anticipating the day I would wear it: the day of the farewell banquet. On that day, hunting season would be opened and guys and girls would be allowed to pair off for the first and last time. I knew one thing for sure: I intended to start a raging fire on that day—with denim, buckles, and snaps!

After several weeks in the camp at El Salvador, the adult staff decided to transfer my half of our team to a village in Guatemala for a building project there. Once again, I marveled at the picturesque scenery and the beautiful people in their colorful, hand-embroidered costumes. I felt especially drawn to the young mothers with long dark braids, their black-eyed "papooses" peeking out from snug bundles attached to their backs.

I thought, *What quiet, reserved people!*—until they went to church. There we discovered that the local Guatemalans had only one volume for singing hymns—excruciatingly, ear-splittingly, loud! We wondered if there was an unannounced competition to see which small, unassuming Guatemalan Christian could puncture the most eardrums. Not only did they have a penchant for singing loud, but they also sang long. My ears rang for hours after every service.

After one of these exhausting services, my ears still ringing and my stomach growling with hunger, I trudged the last few yards alone toward "home." The girl's dorm in Guatemala was actually a two-story adobe house with, praise the Lord, indoor plumbing.

As I have said, I was tired and famished when I happened upon a tree with little green apples. They looked delicious. Reminiscent of Eve, I blatantly ignored one of the "Teen Commandments": Do not eat that which does not abide in a can or a bottle.

I ate of the fruit and I thought I would surely die. Now I know why the songwriter wrote, "God Didn't Make Little Green Apples." It's hard to believe a benevolent, loving God would create something so malevolent. For three days I alternated between agony on my cot and moaning in agony near the, praise the Lord, indoor plumbing.

Then came the good news. We were to board an unaircon-ditioned, unbathroomed bus for a six-hour ride over and under, and over and under, hills and valleys back to our main camp in El Salvador. At the mere thought of it, my stomach lurched.

Then came the *truly* good news. The team leaders felt so sorry for me they declared open season early so I could legally lean on Scott during the journey. And lean I did. The only time he let go of me was when I had to visit the roadside outhouse. When I emerged I promptly passed out into his waiting arms. Sick as I felt, I was delightfully aware of Scott's strong arm around me, his hand caressing mine as he prayed for me to get well.

Miraculously, I began to feel much better even though I was still very weak. We were young and in love and eager to explore the world around us together. Once, in a quaint courtyard, Scott decided to take pictures, and he positioned me among the pigeons strutting about the stone yard.

"Smile, Becky," he coached, "try not to faint for just one minute!"

I still have that snapshot, now framed and displayed in our home. I never want to forget the day when I was fifteen years old, reeling with an intestinal virus among a dozen Spanish-speaking pigeons, and at the same time, euphorically happy.

When we arrived back at home base in El Salvador, I and my stomach settled down. I even managed to be somewhat useful to the work crew for the waning days of the mission. Then, at last, the day of the farewell banquet arrived. That afternoon, I did indeed build a bonfire, and together with my girlfriends, watched the overalls go up in smoke. To my surprise, none of us were overcome by toxic fumes.

After the ceremonial burning of the overalls, I reached into my duffle bag for "The Dress." Scott had bought me a red carnation from a street vendor, so I combed out my dark braids and pinned the flower in my hair. When I stepped out of the chicken shack, my date met me at the door. He was wearing a white Guatemalan shirt and a broad smile of approval.

"Let's go for a walk," he said softly as he reached for my hand. It felt tiny in his strong, yet gentle grip. Together we walked toward the hill overlooking Lake Illapango.

It was supposed to be a romantic walk and it was, except that, with the long dress, I kept falling and stumbling into potholes. Halfway up the hill I gave up the struggle, picked up my skirt, and began trudging up the mountain like an El Salvadoran farmer. I heard Scott laughing behind me.

"You remind me of your mother," he chuckled.

Mother? Hmm-m-m.

At the top of the hill, Scott and I stood together looking down at the foundation our team had somehow managed to complete. We absorbed what would be our last view of the hills and the lake. We would miss it, but we would especially miss the people we had met, our brothers and sisters in Guatemala and those on the team from all over the world.

The evening sun decorated the sky, sending a brilliant burst of purple, red, and orange to celebrate the end of a summer and the beginning of love. Scott turned me to face him, then reached into his pocket and produced a tiny gold band which he slipped on my right ring finger. I later discovered he had bought the ring with all the money he had left, twelve dollars. It was a perfect fit. So were we. Then he kissed me softly for the first time ever, and I thought to myself, *I might as well die and go to heaven right now because I will never be any happier than this on earth.*

A rustle of movement from behind a nearby bush pulled us back to reality, but pleasantly so. Two barefoot El Salvadoran children giggled and darted from behind the bush and down the hill. We laughed with them and reluctantly started back down to the banquet.

Two years later, Scott slipped that very same gold band on my *left* hand. This time he vowed to love, honor, and cherish me as long as he lived, of which I remind him every time I bring home a new dent in the car. My twelve-dollar wedding ring is my most treasured material possession. For our engagement, he gave me a more expensive diamond ring which I lost behind the refrigerator for three years. He lovingly replaced the ring for Christmas. I subsequently sucked it into the vacuum cleaner. Though I found the ring among the lint, the tiny diamond was gone forever.

Since Scott has lost twenty-eight sets of car keys and five pairs of glasses during our marriage, he is not intolerant of my problem. Every Christmas he continues to replace jewelry that we eventually find in the yard, down the drain, or behind a major appliance. But I have prayed for God's eyes to watch over my precious, twelve-dollar wedding band inscribed "Jer. 24:6-7." The memories it represents, and the promise it still holds, are of the most precious gold.

I will build them up and not tear them down;
I will plant them and not uproot them.
I will give them a heart to know me, that I am the Lord.
JEREMIAH 24:6-7

Wedding Ring Worms

I returned from El Salvador by plane (though I probably could have flown without one) and deplaned at Dallas-Fort Worth Airport with Scott much as we had flown away. His folks and mine stood on tiptoe, watching for us to emerge from the plane. We left with a lot of daylight between us, we emerged from the plane as one entity.

Daddy drove me home to our nice brick house on a cul-de-sac in Arlington, Texas, where I had grown up. After weeks in El Salvador, it seemed like the Taj Mahal. I spent so long in the bathtub my toes and fingers turned into twenty prunes.

That evening, the family took Scott and me out for a spaghetti supper, and then we all came back to our house. We spread out on the floor and talked, and talked, and talked. I had come to take this kind of easy communication for granted, hardly remembering what it had been like at our house before the summer of '72.

At that time, the Country Squire panel wagon glinting in the afternoon sun had made the statement to the world that we were "The Arnolds—the Fam" was intact, parked, and stable. But around the olive-green, self-cleaning oven and down the rust shag in the hallway, there was "a whole lot of shakin' goin on" in the hearts of Mom and Dad. There were also quite a few tremors occurring in the nation as a whole.

The sixties had left their mark. Free love changed the 1950s' adage of *Father Knows Best* into the question, "Who *is* my father and *where* did he go?" Something dreadful had happened to Jim and Betty Anderson's America and it was much more serious than little Kathy breaking a window with a baseball. Unbridled freedom had arrived, bringing a total lack of boundaries. Common sense and morality seemed relegated to quaint old black and white reruns. Nothing made much sense anymore.

The women's movement suggested housewives look for fulfillment in outside activity. Mother, not one for being labeled unfulfilled, joined two women's clubs and managed to get elected president of both. Playing bridge provided another outlet for social activity.

Mother continued to run faster and faster in the race for fulfillment. She tells about the day she suddenly realized that when one of us kids wanted to tell her something, we reached out and grabbed her skirt to be sure she stayed still long enough to hear it. Something was haywire. Bridge yielded twenty-six recipes for making anything edible into the shape of a diamond, heart, club, or spade, and the women's clubs caused indelible skin indentions from girdles and high heels, and jaws that ached from forcing a smile when everything was dark and rainy on the inside.

It wasn't long before my parents decided that if there was to be meaning in life, it had to be with God. Each in their own way and their own moment made Jesus first in their hearts and lives. Then the real adventures began in the house on the cul-de-sac in Suburbia.

For one thing, our television played less and less. Mother especially kept an eye on the TV set. She actually made a label for it with her handy little label maker which read, "This television is to be used for the glory of God. Honor Him with your choices." If something came on the screen she felt we shouldn't see, she would leap from her spot at the kitchen sink into the den in a single bound and spread her apron over the screen before we could yell, "Look out, here she comes!"

But seriously, things did change around our home, mostly for the better. As a family we "hung out" more together and spent more time just talking. Mother was always good for one more sloppy joe for a school or church friend. Gradually, our home became a "cool" place to "rap." College students began dropping by for deep theological/philosophical discussions that stretched on until midnight or until Daddy fell asleep and slid out of his recliner, whichever came first.

Daddy often sat for hours in his old rocker in his bedroom, highlighting book after book with a yellow marker—books by such writers as Francis Schaeffer, C. S. Lewis, and Elton True-blood.

Looking back, I realize our home became a kind of substitute coffee house for young people living in turbulent times and faced with tough questions previous generations of Americans had rarely asked. Though most of the talks were over my head, I enjoyed visiting with handsome college men in our living room.

Frequently, serious discussions dissolved into silly, mass hilarity, especially when it got late and our brain cells begged for sleep. If for some reason there had been a police raid, only a breathalyzer would have saved us from a night in jail. It may have also been the effect of sugar-overload, because at that time much of our fellowship centered around food, particularly chocolate. Those are precious memories, and I hope to share evenings like that with my soon-to-be teenagers. I must remember the formula: deep philosophical discussion, late hours, plenty of laughter, and frosted pecan brownies topped with ice cream and hot fudge sauce.

A few months before Scott and I were to marry, my parents called me into their bedroom for a private discussion. Daddy had asked for a leave of absence from his job for several weeks, planning to take the entire family to L'Abri, Francis Schaeffer's community in Switzerland. There, he and Mother planned to study theology and philosophy along with other seekers from around the world.

It sounded great to me. I had always wanted to leap about on top of a Swiss alp, spreading my arms and twirling about in the mountain breeze. I would lift my face toward the sun and break into glorious song, "The hills are alive with the sound of music..."

But Daddy jolted me back to reality with a very tough question.

"Are you sure you want to get married in June before we leave in October," he asked, "or would you consider postponing the wedding for the trip to Switzerland?"

The decision wasn't even hard. I'd just have to belt out my song while I spun around in my new husband's kitchen over a sink of dirty dishes. I was getting married in June! The Arnold Von Trapp family would just have to yodel-lay-he-hoo across Switzerland without big sister's soprano.

Friends and family filled the church on our wedding day that Sunday afternoon in June of 1976. The wedding was like a fairy tale come true, complete with Prince Charming. The fact that we were so young added a Romeo and Juliet quality to the celebration.

Six bridesmaids and groomsmen radiated a pastel haze of color at the front of the church where my white tuxedoed groom waited. I stood in the foyer, dressed in a flowing cloud of white lace and ruffles, my hand resting on Daddy's arm. But my heart rested with the handsome prince waiting for me at the altar.

With the swelling chords of the wedding march, I had the feeling of being carried forward on a wave I could not stop, though it was the moment we had dreamed of for at least two years.

Although I could not have known all that lay ahead (who does?), I knew full well we had made a holy vow in the presence of the living God that afternoon. And when angry words are spoken and thoughts of divorce (or murder) sometimes enter my mind, I think back to that sacred altar and the vows two starry-eyed kids made to each other.

Actually, we managed to remain The Charmings through our entire honeymoon week. Not until we got home did I discover that my handsome prince had a few warts, and the prince began to think perhaps he had accidentally married the wicked step-sister. Thus began the inevitable period of disillusionment, of which all prospective newlyweds are duly warned by their pre-marital counselors, counselors who might as well save their breath. Every engaged couple is sure *their* love will be the exception because no one has ever loved as much as they, not since the beginning of time, nor ever shall again. What we need is post-marital counseling, given about a month after the wedding day when the descent from each other's royal thrones is well underway.

As I recall, the first thing to hit me about newlywed bliss was the 103-degree weather. The only duplex we could afford to rent had no air conditioning. For us, "making whoopee" meant literally shouting, "Whoopee!" every time a breeze found its way through an open window.

Furthermore, Scott hailed from a military family, and I soon learned he liked to make little rules. Now isn't that special? Actually, a number of situations did not turn out as I had dreamed they would.

Disillusionment #1. Scott's heavy work schedule demanded he get adequate rest. This was complicated by (1) the fact that I am a talkative night person, (2) the heat wave, and (3) the fact that our bed had settled into a shape resembling an open hot dog bun due to years of occupancy by previous tenants. These conditions led Scott to make the first rule. He drew an invisible line down the center of the bed and announced that each of us must stick to his or her own side of the bed when it came time to go to sleep.

I tried to follow the instructions, I really did. I hung on to my edge for dear life but I would inevitably roll into the crevice in the center of the bed. When this happened, Scott would grunt and pinch me.

For years I had dreamed of snuggling all night with my honeybee. Instead, I learned he had quite a stinger.

Disillusionment #2. Bathtime is near sacred to me. I love lying in the tub for long periods of time, periodically turning the water on with my toes while leisurely reading a good book.

A few weeks after the honeymoon, Scott suddenly strolled in, interrupting my time and space without so much as a knock, and presented me with a copy of our first month's water bill. He then proceeded to instruct me in the details of how to take a two-minute military shower.

"That's how the Freeman family does it," he finished.

Now, I might have handled the hot dog bun rule with grace, but nobody—NOBODY—messes with my bath! He soon discovered that even small honeybees can pack a stinger, too.

Disillusionment #3. Quite a few of our difficulties seemed to center around the basic problem of obtaining nourishment. I was fairly new to the art of cooking, but I felt comfortable with Mother's tortilla chicken casserole recipe. In an effort to avoid heating up the kitchen later in the day, I prepared the dish early in the morning and left it on the stove all day, waiting for our dinner that evening.

I was shocked when Scott refused to eat my first homemade meal because of a silly worry about botulism or something. I threw the casserole *and* the beautiful baking dish (a wedding gift) in the trash. If he wasn't going to eat my dinner, I certainly was not going to wash the pan.

Our fights became so spectacular that I began giving them titles; more than a few of them had to do with meals. One in particular I dubbed, "The Salad Fight."

I had made a delicious three-course meal, but Scott complained about the lack of Thousand Island dressing on the table (the Arnold Family is blue cheese). As any dutiful wife would do, I quickly whipped up some homemade dressing, poured it on his salad, picked up the dish, and walked out the door to dump the entire concoction on the hood of his car. He in turn jumped up, ran outside, and washed the mess off the car with a water hose, then followed me into the house with the hose.

Then there was the "I Can Walk Home Faster Than You" fight. For this round, we decided to eat out, and one might think that would have eased the chances of another bout. However, we had a fuss in the car on the way to the restaurant, and each determined to play the martyr and walk home. We spent some time tossing the keys back and forth like a game of hot potato; the keys ended up on the pavement between us. We took off in a dead heat race-walk, huffing and puffing down Main Street until we both ran out of breath. We eventually made up out of sheer exhaustion.

That was our first year. In between our battles royale, we had some great times, too. Somebody with a twisted mind gifted us with a pet chinchilla which we dubbed Wilbur, and, like the children we were, we enjoyed letting him run loose in the duplex. However, when we needed to put him in his cage, we discovered what a fast little bugger he was. We chased him with coats and blankets, trying to get close enough to catch him in one without hurting him, but usually we were laughing so hard we gave up and left him to his own devices in our little duplex.

We planned all our college classes together so that I could ride with Scott on the back of his motorcycle—to Mother's terror. We were almost always late, and I'm sure we made quite a scene roaring down the highway while I held on to Scott with one hand and tried to keep the hot rollers in my hair with the other.

Winter came, bringing with it a rare Texas snow. It was great fun to build a snowman and to chase each other with snowballs. For our P.E. requirement, we learned square dancing because it was the only possible athletic activity we could do together. I was delighted to discover that my husband was as graceful as he was handsome, and we both loved dancing together—until the inevitable happened and he stepped on my toe and broke it.

In our first spring we planted a garden, and, like good Earth People, tried to avoid using insecticides. We read in the *Organic Gardener* that insects are repulsed by the odor of their own kind, so we experimented with several formulas for non-toxic insect repellent, each containing organically hand smashed bugs as the active ingredient. Then we tried picking the bugs off by hand.

We had planted thirty-two tomato plants which yielded 320 plump tomatoes, our best crop. We were thrilled until we realized neither of us liked tomatoes.

In our third year, Scott finished his degree, but fourteen springs would pass before I earned mine. After three years of work toward a degree in Music Education, I dropped out because I wanted to have a baby. As hard as it is to believe, we had a little trouble getting the project under way, but once I got the hang of it...

[Love] always protects, always trusts, always hopes,
always perseveres. Love never fails.
1 CORINTHIANS 13:7-8
∾

———

SEVEN

Worm with a View

I was a new bride suffering from a bad case of homesickness when I began receiving Mother's blue tissue letters from Huemoz, Switzerland. The first one read:

Dearest Scott and Becky:

Your Daddy thinks he's died and gone to heaven, studying every day in the chapel overlooking a breathtaking view of the Rhone Valley below.

That's okay, Mom. Rub it in. I, on the other hand, am overlooking a breathtaking view of unbelievably smelly laundry as I wait for my twentieth load of clothes to dry at the corner laundromat.

At noon, the budding philosophers gather in small groups at various chalets where they enjoy simple meals and complicated conversations with people from all over the world.

Scott and I are enjoying complicated meals—trying to figure out just what it is I have cooked for dinner—and simple conversations such as, "This really tastes gross, Honey," and "Shut up and eat, Sweetheart."

In the afternoon, everyone works around the community, but it is simple work, such as gardening or housekeeping.
Did she define gardening and housework as simple!?

And me? I'm a stranger in a strange land when it comes to daily shopping in the French-speaking villages. The French are not noted for friendliness and warmth toward people who do not speak French. I, being a people person, have often had my feelings hurt.
I know exactly what you mean. When I go to the bakery at Piggly Wiggly and order a "Kro-sahwn," the lady just stares at me.

Our first encounter with Dr. Schaeffer helped a great deal, because he was so kind and personal in his lectures. Daddy and I, along with David and Rachel, often gather with others in the chapel for discussions with him. He's a small man with collar-length gray hair and a goatee. He wears knickers most of the time. The first evening, he sat on the rock hearth, smiled, and asked simply, "Where would you like to begin?"

Something unusual has happened in reference to our accommodations. As you know, we're staying in several rented rooms in a converted saw mill called the Rose Farm.

Yes, I remember. With Grandpa and little Luke, was it?

Well, the proprietors left for England and asked us to take care of renting out other rooms to L'Abri visitors. We find we're duplicating our discussion nights in Texas, but with friends from around the world.
Good thing the Swiss are noted for their chocolate.

A young family from Australia rents three rooms of the Rose Farm. I served them a good ol' Texas barbecue dinner, which their four-year-old Johnny referred to as "bah be que tea."

David has entered into a new stage of contentment, having found a small boy to aggravate. Would you believe David has a job harvesting grapes in the vineyard? Your little sister's summer job is also impressive. She's herding cows at Bonzon farm.

Well, that's certainly a departure from flipping burgers and pizzas.

Rachel may have left an interesting impression about Americans on a French gendarme.

I hate to show my ignorance, but what the Sam Hill is a gendarme? One of her cows, maybe?

One morning after lacing her hiking boots and double tying the knot, she discovered she had a bee in one of her boots. As she began the fastest un-lacing job on record, she heard an insistent knock on the door. Hopping across the floor, still unlacing as she hopped, she opened the door to see the stern face of the gendarme, who rattled off something in French.

So much for the cow theory.

It was quite a scene as she frantically gestured to her boot, making buzzing sounds like a bee, indicating to him that she didn't speak his language. He, in order to help her understand, spoke louder. I'm not sure she ever found out what his business was at the Rose Farm, but she took care of the first order of business—the bee came out of her boot somewhat worse for wear. She did not wait two seconds for revenge.

I'm assuming the gendarme was somewhat less insistent after that display.

The letter ended with love and inquiries about how Scott and I were getting along as man and wife, and how we liked college and our little white duplex. I let the paper-thin airmailed letter fall to my lap and sighed as I daydreamed of Heidi and goat's-milk cheese. It all sounded so Old World and interesting. How I did miss them!

Both of us especially missed the traditional Sunday lunches at my family's house after church. For some reason, Scott's longing for one of my mother's homecooked meals had increased passionately. But at least the weather had cooled, and I eventually managed to serve a piece of meat resembling a Sunday pot roast. And with time, Scott and I began to find a new closeness. We realized that we were becoming a family on our own, just the two of us.

A few weeks later, I realized just how serious my father's quest in Switzerland was. He had been considering leaving industry, to enter seminary to prepare for full-time ministry. Several people at L'Abri had encouraged him to go ahead with the idea. A visit in the home of Edith Schaeffer helped him make the final decision. Mother wrote details of that afternoon:

Mrs. Schaeffer opened the door of Chalet Le Melez, her warm smile welcoming Daddy and me for our afternoon appointment. I recall thinking, *This is a very pretty lady!* as the petite, delicate-boned woman directed us to a sofa in the softly lighted room. Outside, mist had settled over the mountains, but inside, the fire crackled its own welcome as Mrs. Schaeffer chatted quietly and poured tea into china cups. She made a charming picture, her long, dark hair pulled into a thick bun at the back of her head. A few grey strands added softness to a face that was aging gracefully.

She asked where we were from and how we were faring at L'Abri, and if there were anything she might do to make our stay all that we had hoped it would be.

This is a very nice lady, I decided as your dad began to explain to her his thoughts about leaving his job and going to seminary.

"How old are your children, George?" she asked.

"The two still at home are twelve and fourteen," he responded. Then Edith began to talk about their years in the work at L'Abri, and about its tremendous rewards, but also about its sacrifices.

"It was not easy for our children to almost always have guests in our home. If we had it to do over again," she smiled ruefully, "we would take more time off to be together, just with our family. Your children are at such a crucial age. What you are considering would mean a lot of change for your teenagers.

"There are many opportunities for ministry open for laymen that wouldn't require so much upheaval in your family. You may want to consider something of that sort for the time being, and think of full-time ministry when your children are on their own."

At the end of our thirty-minute appointment, we prepared to leave. Our hostess cheerfully ignored our preparations and two hours later, she walked us to the door and took thirty more minutes to say goodbye.

Your dad and I walked silently together down the mountain toward the Rose Farm each thinking our own thoughts. Finally, I broke the silence.

"Honey, we'll only get one chance at raising our kids."

"I know," he answered quietly. We reached the porch of the Rose Farm and he put his arm around me, pulling me close to him. "For now, I'm convinced—our *family* is our ministry."

Early in November, Mom, Dad, David, and Rachel dropped out of the sky at Dallas-Fort Worth airport, back into our arms with a bounce and a tumble, almost as if they had not been gone. The chocolate-covered discussion/comedy nights resumed, but with a new make up of our family. Scott and I were now enrolled in a Christian college, and he had especially come alive to history, to Schaeffer's writings, and to philosophy. It was great fun to observe my husband and my parents becoming even closer friends than before.

That is not to say there were no adjustments. No indeedy. We still laugh about our first camping trip together. One beautiful morning in South Carolina, Scott loaded the van while

Mother was in the bath house. As one might expect, Scott's idea of a tidy loading job and my mother's idea were as far removed from each other as the east is from the west, to borrow a phrase.

After an exchange of words that soon grew testy, we all climbed into the van and drove toward breakfast in stony silence. Once inside the cafe, we each ordered a hearty meal, and the waitress returned to the kitchen to fetch it. A minute later, Scott swallowed hard, excused himself and went out to the parking lot. Mother followed quickly behind him, dabbing at her eyes. I sat in the booth a minute or two longer, blinking back tears until I had to give it up and head for the ladies' room.

Daddy still laughs at the look on the waitress' face when she came to the table barely able to carry all the plates of food we had ordered and found one customer to eat it all.

There have been a few other scrapes over the years, most of which we can laugh about, and one or two which are filed under, "Painful—Handle with Care." But not long ago, after a fishing trip with Daddy and our boys, Scott characterized Daddy as a "best friend." And as for Mother, if anybody went after Scott to do him bodily harm, they would have to go over her first. And I think that might include me.

He will turn the hearts of the fathers to their children,
and the hearts of the children to their fathers.
MALACHI 4:6
&

EIGHT

Yummy Worms

My struggles in the kitchen continued for more years. Some days I was lucky just to find a clean pan. Because weenies cook faster than any other cut of meat and can be prepared in such a variety of ways, I gained the reputation of being the Weenie Queen. Weenies can be barbecued, beaned, or bunned in less than ten minutes. (The one drawback of any food is that it can also be burned.) This tended to be my preparation of choice, (not really by choice), and my budding family came to expect it. One morning I noticed five-year-old Zeke busily scraping a perfectly browned piece of toast over the trash can.

"Zeke, honey," I interrupted, "I didn't burn your toast today. You don't have to scrape it."

"Oh," he replied in surprise, "I thought we always had to whittle the toast."

Not long after that, I stepped into the kitchen to find it filled with smoke, our dinner a blackened ruin. At that moment, Zach strolled nonchalantly into the kitchen.

"M-m-m-m," he remarked, "smells like Mom's home cooking."

Sometimes I worry that my children will be invited to someone else's outdoor barbeque, by-pass the food, and pig-out on the charcoal.

Since I am told that confession is good for the soul, I feel compelled to confess one of the worst results I have ever had from a dish that I created. It was a horrible day when I realized that I had actually killed Zeke's pet with a casserole.

It began when Zeke left his pet ferret in my care for a few days while he went to visit my mother. She had volunteered to keep the children while I took a mini-course at East Texas State University. I tried to get comfortable with Mousequat, who was cute and fun to watch, but unfortunately smelled like stinky feet on a warm day. He also enjoyed taking playful but painful nips at our fingers at unpredictable intervals, a habit which made me more than a little nervous.

Choosing to conquer my ambivalent feelings toward Mousequat, I picked up a copy of the Ferret Lover's Brochure, although I realized that, realistically, my affections toward him would probably only reach the level of Ferret liker. I was not surprised to read that ferrets enjoy eating people food. Since I happened to have some leftovers in the fridge, I decided to give Mousequat a special treat—a generous portion of my Mexican casserole. I watched him eat enthusiastically, and feeling proud of my benevolence, I placed him gingerly back in his cage with nary a missing phalange on either of my hands.

The ferret brochure failed to mention one important item— ferrets cannot burp. The next morning Zeke returned and went to check on Mousequat. The animal was deceased, mysteriously swollen from the size of a paper towel tube to that of a hairy watermelon with eyes. An autopsy was required to eliminate the possibility of some contagious and fatal disease, and when the vet called with the results, I felt like a murderer. The verdict? Death by Mexican casserole gas.

Only we parents who have inadvertently run over or poisoned our child's pet can understand the kind of guilt and pain that comes with this experience. For weeks I could not bear to ask Zeke to so much as take out the trash. I was afraid he'd flash those sad brown eyes at me as if to say, "I may be in therapy when I'm thirty years old coping with the lack of trust in all my significant relationships, and you are asking me to take out the trash?"

Thankfully, Zeke took out his grief in the form of a letter to Bill Wallace, best-selling author of Zeke's favorite adventure books including *Beauty*, *Red Dog*, and, ironically, *Ferrets in the Bedroom, Lizards in the Fridge*. I will be forever grateful to this wonderful ex-teacher and principal turned children's writer, for helping to get me off the hook with the following letter to Zeke:

Dear Zeke:

I was sorry to hear about your ferret. But I wanted you to know that I *do* understand.

When I was about ten or so, my dad got me an Indigo Snake. (They are sort of an indigo blue color, but so dark that they look almost black.) I always liked snakes and he was real gentle—never tried to bite or anything like that. He was a great pet.

When I was twelve, I went to a boy's camp near Kerrville, Texas, called Rio Vista. While I was gone, Mom and Dad were "supposed" to take care of my snake. I was at camp for a month and after they picked me up, on the drive home, they told me that my snake had died. When I asked them what happened to it, they said they fed it a horny-toad and it must have gotten stuck or something.

It made me mad, because I knew you couldn't feed that snake horny-toads. I'd done it a couple of times, because that's all I could find to feed him, but I always watched to make sure he swallowed it head first. (That way the sharp horns fold down and don't puncture the snake's insides.) My snake probably swallowed it tail-first, and they didn't watch him. After thinking about it, I figured Mom and Dad probably just didn't know.

I guess I did a bunch of dumb stuff, too. I was always breaking things or doing something I wasn't supposed to (seems like I always got caught, too). But Mom and Dad were pretty good about forgiving me when I did dumb stuff. I figured the best thing to do was forgive them like they always seemed to forgive me.

Like I said, I understand how you feel. Hope you can forgive your mom. Sometimes, parents aren't much smarter than we are—but at least it sounds like she was trying to do the right thing.

Your friend,

Bill*

Obviously, this man cares about kids and I plan to buy every book he ever writes. And yes, I'm forgiven. We can even joke about it some now. Zeke got mad at Zachary not long ago and asked me if I had some leftover Mexican casserole he could feed his brother.

Now comes the truly amazing part of this chapter. Believe it or not, I found myself looking down the gun barrel of an absurd destiny. I would one day become a food caterer.

Sacrifices and . . . burnt offerings . . . you did not desire, nor were you pleased with them.

HEBREWS 10:8

*Used by permission

Wormy Puppies

Our dogs have eaten so many of the children's pet chicks and bunnies that I have a generic name for them: Dog Food.

I have learned not to get attached to pets, except perhaps an occasional dog. I recently read an article entitled, "Endangered Species: Millions of dogs and cats vanish every year. Will yours be next?" I'm ashamed to confess, my sinful nature leaped with hope.

Like all mothers when confronted by their child holding a puppy in their arms and begging with heart and soul to be allowed to keep it, I at first refuse to even *think* about it. Gradually, however, I am worn down, and they are allowed to keep the animal, with the standard provision.

"*You* are going to be the one to take care of him. *Do you hear me?* You've got to feed him, and keep him *outside!* And if he makes a single mess in the house, he's a goner and you may be, too!"

The standards are rigorously met for about a week, but by the end of the second week, the dog thinks your king size bed was installed just for him. Furthermore, if Momma didn't feed him, the animal would starve. Because Momma is the one who feeds him most, the animal has become attached to her, and inevitably, vice versa. I know this not only from personal experience but also from memories of pets that I and my siblings were supposed to take care of as we grew up.

Most of the time, our pets were cats, most notably a homely tri-colored female named Midnight and a handsome figure of a male we called Wallace. But my brother David was the cat charmer in the family, and, unless Midnight was in a family way (homely or not, she always seemed to find husbands), I did not generally become emotionally involved with the cats. They so obviously preferred David I knew it could only end in heartbreak.

On one occasion, Mother was in a hurry to leave the house for an appointment and quickly started the station wagon for the trip. As she drove down the drive, she heard a terrible commotion—an unnerving series of bumps and howls—howls she recognized as being feline, and probably coming from Midnight.

Just as Mother was about to go in the house and call Daddy to see if it would hurt the car to drive it with a cat in the fan belt, Midnight shot out from under the car, a one-inch strip of hair neatly shaved down the entire length of her back.

Soon after, Midnight took up residence elsewhere, and within a year, David brought Wallace home. He gazed beseechingly at Mother holding the yellow kitten in his arms. The story had the usual ending.

"You are going to take care of him. *Do you hear me?*"

By this time, we had been through several cats, and after one of them had decided he much preferred a nice, soft, carpeted corner of the bedroom to a litter box, his successors seemed to think this entitled them to the same privilege. With Wallace, David was given to understand that he had better teach him to use a litter box, and that every single mishap would be David's responsibility.

When the inevitable happened, Mother dispatched David to the bedroom corner with paper towels, soapy water, and a scrub brush. She assumed all was going as it should. However, she walked into the kitchen a few minutes later to observe David at the kitchen sink watching the garbage disposal. A strange odor filled the room. So intent was he that he jumped when Mother yelped in horror, her worst fears confirmed.

"Huh? What!" David responded, trying to figure out what all the fuss was about. After all, garbage is garbage, isn't it?

After Wallace went to cat heaven, I began to lay the groundwork for getting a pet of my own to love. I was not about to consider a cat, knowing I couldn't compete with David for its affection, but I began to read the newspaper ads to see what kind of puppies might be "free to a good home." I persuaded Mother that it was *my* turn to have a pet, since all the cats had ended up being David's. Besides, my fourteenth birthday was coming up and I couldn't think of another thing I wanted except a puppy.

At last, her sense of guilt conquered, we acquired a six-week old, half-breed Pomeranian. When we brought him home, Mother decided he looked like a thistle, a round ball of blonde fur with limpid Pomeranian eyes staring out at us. I named him Angel, Rachel named him Po Po, and David named him Weezer. It's no small wonder he was confused from the start.

We began the process of trying to housebreak the new puppy, but he couldn't quite seem to grasp what we had in mind. If he had not been adorable, he would have been gone. He was even allowed to stay on after he pulled his crowning stunt.

Mother had trimmed the fat off a ham and placed the trimmings in a plastic bag in the trash under the sink. She then left home for several hours, leaving Po Po to his own devices.

When she returned and walked in the front door, Po Po came bounding joyfully to meet her, a little heavy on his feet. In fact, he was about twice as round as he had been when Mother left a few hours earlier. Not only that, what little remained of the ham trimmings were strewn across the kitchen into the living room. About the time Mother grasped what had happened, Po Po keeled over at her feet.

You might think she would have felt it served him right, but she had a weakness for sick or injured animals. She grabbed him up, ran to the car, and roared to the vet's office, taking the corners on two wheels, not knowing if Po Po was alive or dead. She charged into the pet doctor's examining room, explaining as she went.

When she laid Po Po on the vet's examining table, he struggled woozily to his feet, and after a shot of morphine, got to spend the night in style at the animal hospital. After paying the bill, Mother was careful to remember that even though Po Po was too dumb to potty train, he was smart enough to open the kitchen cabinet with his paw and get into the trash.

As for me, I had imagined that Angel-Weezer-Po Po would follow me about the house, snuggle in my arms, sleep at the foot of my bed, and learn to love me above all others. However, he had a tendency to run the other direction when he saw me coming, and I *could* hold him in my arms, but I had to face him away from me and ignore the growling and snapping that went on. I was the only member of the family so honored, and the family would hoot and howl at the spectacle while I insisted, "See? He just *loves* me!"

He was not without his redeeming features, however, and we still laugh about some of his weird antics. We could take a towel, drag it on the floor in front of him and he would immediately latch onto it with his teeth, flatten out like a platypus, and allow us to pull him all over the house, which sent the entire family into hysterics.

He had deeply-ingrained sheep-herding instincts and spent many happy hours trying to herd beetles across our patio, his nose to the concrete as if it were the most important task in the world. Unfortunately, he had the same tendency to herd cars on busy streets every time he managed to sneak out a carelessly opened door.

Other larger, wiser dogs would have been terrified at the cars whizzing by at peak traffic time, but not Po Po. You would have thought he was a traffic cop, the way he worked the middle of the street. Usually, someone in our neighborhood who had come to know who this half-witted half-breed belonged to would call, and we would risk life and limb to dash into the traffic and drag him home.

Po Po had a number of besetting sins. If we had guests, he was so deliriously happy to see them that he made it almost impossible for *us* to visit with them. If we put him outside when guests were coming, he ran back and forth across the yard, barking a high-pitched bark that drove the neighbors to contemplate giving him a ground glass hamburger patty.

Po Po dearly loved sneaking out any open door and, on two occasions, Mother had to post signs on telephone posts and in grocery stores and pay a ten dollar reward to get him back.

One morning, I was standing with a group of friends on the high school grounds waiting for the bell to ring. I looked up to see Po Po bouncing across the grounds toward me with Mother in hot pursuit behind him wearing a bright red robe and curlers in her hair. I pretended I didn't know either of them and dashed into the building.

Meanwhile, Po Po was approaching two years old and was not yet potty trained, which is all right for a child but not for a dog. He was too dumb to potty train, yet after he had soiled the carpet, he would stand just inside the door of the room, peek around the corner, and watch for Mother to come after him with the newspaper.

Po Po's failings eventually ended his membership in our family. We were at wits end about his failure to accomplish the most elemental of skills, and we were about to get a houseful of new carpet. What to do, what to do!

On the day the carpet was to be installed, I went out the door to go to school and left it open, as I almost always did. Po Po was out the door like a shot. Mother responded in her usual way.

"Grab him, Becky! PO PO, COME BACK HERE!" and she ran for the car keys, wearing her red robe and curlers, while I cringed. As Po Po rounded the corner, she skidded to a stop at the car, leaned against it and watched him disappear from sight. For a moment she seemed lost in thought. Then she calmly found the house slipper she had lost on the way to the car, walked back into the house, shut the door, and poured herself a cup of coffee.

We always hoped Po Po found his way to a good home where people knew better than we did how to train half-witted, beautiful little dogs. He was so charming that we had no doubt he would find a good home, at least for a while.

My husband has given his heart to one—and only one—dog. Their story is bittersweet.

In the rural area where we lived, a little boy had been bitten by a wild puppy, and in order for the boy to avoid painful rabies shots, Scott found himself facing the terrible chore of finding the litter of puppies, destroying them and sending them to the state capitol for testing.

Scott took his gun and did what had to be done. It was much like the tearful scene from "Old Yeller." As he finished the hateful job, the stray mother of the pups walked to Scott, gazed sadly at the gun barrel, waiting with resignation. The executioner wiped away a tear, stooped down and put his arms around the little mutt and tenderly apologized, stroking her rough fur.

From that moment, she became his faithful, loving "Lady," following him everywhere he went and being rewarded royally with the choicest of morsels. But then, as animal stories so often end, he accidentally ran over her two years later. He buried her near the edge of a lake in one of her favorite resting spots. For the next few days when I looked out the window I often saw Scott sitting near her grave, his head on his knees.

I'll leave it to theologians to debate whether or not animals have souls. Yet, I have always believed that since Heaven is full of everything wonderful, God will have the pets we came to love waiting there to welcome us. Don't you?

But the poor man had nothing
except one little ewe lamb he had bought.
He raised it, and it grew up with him and his children.
It shared his food, drank from his cup and even slept in his
arms. It was like a daughter to him.

2 SAMUEL 12:3

Wander Worms

M y sister Rachel and I are just concluding a long distance
telephone conversation. It is 1983, and she has called
from her college dorm in Kansas to my parents' house in Texas.
There are moving boxes all around me.

"It's going to be especially hard for you to let them go, I
know," she sympathized.

"I can hardly stand to think about it," I responded. "But I
guess they know what they're doing."

This kind of conversation usually takes place among parents
of college-aged kids who have decided to see the world on a
bicycle and a shoe string. In our case, however, we were discussing our forty-five-year-old parents. Daddy quit a secure job in
aerospace and accepted an unlikely position as director of
Academic Services at a Christian university in Virginia. Never

mind that he had never worked in academia or ministry before. He had always dreamed of it, and now it looked like he was going to do it. At a third less salary. And, he was planning to take the grandmother of my children with him.

I felt a strange parental concern, as if my traditional mother and father were suddenly buying lovebeads and a Harley—off to make peace, not war.

There in my parents' empty house, I said good-bye to Rachel and slowly unplugged the phone and placed it in a cardboard box for the movers. The time had come for Daddy to begin another adventure. This time it would be Virginia, over fifteen hundred miles away.

It might as well be Europe again, I thought sadly. *Except this time, they won't be coming back soon.*

My folks pulled out of the driveway after several heart-rending embraces and farewells. Scott and I had volunteered to do some last minute cleanup in the house on the cul-de-sac in Suburbia. It was now a huge empty shell with nothing but floods of childhood memories bouncing off every freshly painted wall and undraped window.

Zachary was four at the time and couldn't understand where his beloved grandparents were going and why their house had nothing in it. Zeke, at two, realized that even the toy box in the hall closet was gone.

"Mommy," Zach asked with moisture glistening on his long dark lashes, "let's pray for Jesus to bring Granny and Daddy George back to their house now."

I grabbed him in a bear hug before he could see my tears spill down my face and onto his soft knit shirt.

Yes, it was going to be very hard to let them go.

When my parents moved to Virginia, a friend gave them a verse of Scripture, Malachi 4:2, "You will go forth and skip about like calves from the stall" (NASB). From the sound of Mother's voice over the long distance wire, the prophet had proved to be one hundred percent correct. It hadn't taken them any time at all to begin kicking up their respective hooves.

"Becky," she giggled, "Daddy and I have done it again! You know we're looking for a church home here. Well, last Sunday we visited a lovely, mission-oriented Sunday School class. They were discussing a dinner they were going to prepare for a group from Jungle Aviation and Radio Service, and they were looking for volunteers to help with the meal. When several people responded, the announcer said, 'We really appreciate you helping to cook and serve those people in JAARS.'"

"Now I ask you. Could *you* have kept a straight face?"

The laughter we shared eased the ache in my heart from knowing they were no longer close by where I could drop by with the kids. To further lift my spirits, I hung up the phone and decided to take Zach and Zeke to the mall for lunch.

I headed for the cafeteria where Mother and I used to meet for lunch on an almost weekly basis to talk and coo over the grandbabies. As I pushed two toddler-filled highchairs through the line, the uniformed lady on the other side of the counter asked, "Would you like a salad?" It was a simple question, really.

Mother and I always split a spinach salad, an order of fish and, of course, chocolate pie. Who would share my lunch this day? My two and three-year-old sons were *not* fish and spinach lovers.

In full view of several surprised blue-haired ladies, I pulled Zach and Zeke out of their highchairs, swallowed the lump in my throat and decided we'd better go to the corn dog booth instead.

A couple of weeks later, Mother wrote of *her* first experience with lunch alone at a cafeteria in Virginia. She had forced herself to go through the line, but as she pushed her tray along, an elderly lady moved along just ahead of her. When the woman neared the cash register, the cashier looked at her and at Mother.

"Are you two together?" she asked.

The elderly lady looked startled and answered, "Oh no! All my friends are dead."

Mother said she almost wailed, "And all *my* friends are in Texas!"

At the corn dog stand, I wiped ketchup and mustard off the boys and supplied each with a lollipop. I then moved steadily down the mall, children in tow, trying not to think of Mother. But then I passed a dress shop, and found myself suppressing a giggle as another "mother story" began to elbow its way into my mind.

On a warm summer afternoon, Mother was hurriedly shopping for a pair of walking shorts at the largest and most elegant mall in the city. The moving van was on its way to the house in Arlington to haul their belongings to Virginia. Time was of the essence. She developed a system of grabbing three or four pair of shorts from the rack, running into the dressing room and trying them on, throwing her lightweight jersey skirt back on, running out and grabbing more shorts, and returning to the dressing room.

She finally found a pair she liked, ran back to the rack to return the rejects, and noticed a young serviceman looking her over with interest.

Hmmm, old girl, she thought to herself, *maybe you haven't lost all your charm yet!* She dashed to the cash register stand, which happened to face broad doors leading into the length of the mall. As she made out her check, a woman moved close to her, her eyes wide in horror.

"Did you know your skirt is up in back?" she whispered. When Mother checked, the entire back of her skirt was rolled up neatly around the waist band. No wonder the young soldier had been intrigued.

Still smiling to myself, I was yanked back to the present world by a scream of outrage from Zeke. Thinking he must surely have lost a leg in an escalator, I felt somewhat relieved to discover he was staring in disbelief at an empty lollipop stick. Zach observed Zeke's outburst with both cheeks bulging, his eyes oozing innocence.

Taking my life in my hands, I went in after one of the candies and popped it into Zeke's gaping maws with nary a thought for germs. Peace descended, and Zach decided to steer the subject away from his "breaking and entering" charge.

"Can we go fwimmin' when we get home?" he asked. My mind wandered from taking the boys swimming, to swimsuits in general, to a specific swimming suit—a green bikini—worn with fur-lined boots. Another Mother story.

This time we were vacationing at Holly Lake, our favorite family vacation spot in the piney woods of East Texas. One morning Mother decided to enjoy her coffee on the porch of our rented mobile home. We kids disappeared into the woods to do our own thing, and she propped up her feet, soaking up the peace and quiet. Before long, a small dog, which looked more like a rag mop than a dog, frolicked down the path, up onto the porch and gave Mother his "jumpin', lickin', dawg" greeting. Scarcely had she wiped the slobber off her feet when the dog's mistress fell into view, breathless with apology as she attempted to corner her "naughty boy."

Mother guessed the woman to be about her age, but while Mother was clad in her robe and no makeup, this lady was clad (just barely) in a lime-green bikini and fur-lined boots. The extent of her tan indicated the bikini was her most frequent costume, which indicated to Mother that they might not have a lot in common. Even so, they struck up a conversation in which Mother became the primary listener.

The topic fell upon the lady's daughter, of whom she was extremely proud because she worked as a hostess in a famous nightclub (now defunct) in Dallas where she was required to wear a small costume resembling a small rabbit. Mother's new acquaintance expected to marry again soon, and her fiancé had a motto: "You can tell a successful man by how expensive his toys are." Furthermore, she owned her own business in Dallas, and she knew the score.

"I don't hire young, cute women," she declared, "They're nothing but trouble in an office. They fuss with each other and the men can't keep their minds on their work. I hire ugly, old, women." She then shrewdly looked Mother over, sized her up and paid her the supreme compliment: "I'd hire you."

My mouth turned up at the corners recalling how many times we three kids had teased our pretty mother about being an "ugly old woman" as a result of that famous encounter. Every time she repeated the story, she laughed hardest of all.

Sighing, I gave up on the mall and loaded my sticky, tired, whiney kids into the car and drove home. Happily, a letter from Virginia waited in the mailbox.

Once I had the boys down for a nap, I poured myself a cup of hazelnut-flavored coffee, and settled down in a rocker to read the letter while I "celebrated the moments of my life." Unless you are a mother of two pre-schoolers who are down for a nap, you will never understand the true ecstasy of a moment of quiet, a cup of coffee, and something interesting to read.

Dearest Scott, Becky, Zach, and Zeke,

Though we ache to see you all, it helps to have Rachel living with us now. Your little sister likes Virginia so well, she says we can go back to Texas if we want to—she's staying!

We are coming to love Virginia, though. We're an hour's drive from colonial Williamsburg and you know how much Daddy loves "hysterical markers." He also enjoys his work at the university—using his business skills and enjoying deep fellowship with other believers. I'm enjoying being more involved in your dad's work than I could be when he was in industry. I'm leading the University Women's Organization, which is fine. I really enjoy working with women. In fact, I love women. Of course, I love men, too. And kids aren't too bad when they're cleaned up.

Our little twenty-year-old bungalow overlooks a tree-filled yard and a gorgeous lake! The only problem is that we only have one bathroom. This is causing some stress in our marriage because Daddy rarely remembers to adjust the faucet back to "bath" after his showers, and I rarely remember to check it until I am on my hands and knees to clean out the tub and fill it for my bath. When I turn the faucet on, I am immediately doused and you know how I hate to wash my well-sprayed hairdo more than once a week!

We're still looking for a church home. Last Wednesday evening we visited another church and arrived during a video series on marriage. Since we've been at our marriage quite a while, I had a little trouble paying attention. At the end of the video, a questionnaire was passed out about the material just covered. I left mine in my lap, but Daddy began to fill his in by reflex. I gouged him in the ribs with my elbow.

"Good grief, George!" I whispered. "We've been married almost thirty years. What are you doing filling that out?"

He grinned, but finished the questionnaire. Church was dismissed and we returned home to our bungalow, where I proceeded to get ready for bed by starting my bath water, and your father went to the bedroom to turn down the covers. Once again, he had left the shower lever on, and I caught it full blast on my teased bun. Catching my breath, I rocked back on my heels and yelled, "I want a divorce!"

After a moment of silence, I heard a tap on the bathroom door, and opened it to find Daddy standing there in his pajamas, already cuddling his bedtime pillow. His expression was holy, if not holier than thou.

"If you had filled out your questionnaire like *I* did," he said ever so kindly, "that wouldn't have bothered you."

I must confess, I almost bludgeoned him to death with his own feather pillow.

By the way, Rachel is dating a tall, slender, young man with a shock of dark hair, nice blue eyes and a jaunty nose. His name is Scott St.John-Gilbert, no less.

I folded the letter and laughed out loud. Only my mother, a true writer, would use the word "jaunty" to describe someone's nose. A true word nut and reigning family champion of Scrabble,™ she recently described herself as having trouble "ambulating" without her glasses.

"Mother," I said to her over the miles, "why is it that other people simply *walk* while you insist on *"ambulating"*? With that thought, I jauntily ambulated out of my rocker, refreshed by the news and the giver thereof.

My parents remained and prospered in Virginia for nearly three years. During this time, I gave birth to Rachel Praise. They came to Texas for her birth, and we managed to see them fairly often, but we made huge sacrifices to be together.

Daddy's job, though rewarding, was beginning to take its toll. I was amused by the latest story Mother shared via Ma Bell.

During Daddy's career in industry, he had worked with programs involving millions of dollars, yet he almost always had been able to leave problems at the office at the end of the day and sleep like a baby. However, the first outdoor commencement and reception he supervised almost put him under.

He had scheduled the celebration to be out-of-doors, but nature had scheduled a hurricane not far away. The weatherman predicted high winds for their area. Daddy and his committee debated about what to do and finally decided to pray a lot and go ahead as planned.

"During the reception," Mother wrote, "I saw at least one paper plate filled with barbecue and potato salad become airborne and land smack in the back of a lady's head."

Later came the lighting of the Eternal Flame. The chancellor of the university was supposed to do this, but it eventually took Daddy, a professor, and a blow torch to accomplish the task.

The university has an annual spiritual awareness event called "Seven Days Ablaze," in which the pace equals any Daddy ever knew in industry. By the end of the week, Daddy came home dragging his coat, his tie untied, and generally looking to be on his last leg.

"I hate to make a negative confession," he told Mother, "but the registrar has crashed and burned during Seven Days Ablaze."

At the end of three years, my parents felt the Lord was calling them to, as Steve and Annie Chapman sing, "Turn Their Hearts Toward Home." There were several signals. First of all, it began to be obvious that my grandparents' time on earth was nearing an end. Our Nonnie had suffered a heart attack and stroke, Grandad Arnold had to have his carotid arteries reamed out, and Grandmother Arnold had been diagnosed with Alzheimer's disease.

When Daddy's former employer offered him a good job back in Texas, I was thrilled. I had recently discovered that baby number four was on its way and I felt a renewed need to have my parents close. There is indeed a time to be born and a time to die, and it is a great blessing to be surrounded by loved ones for either event.

It may be that Zach made the final impact upon their decision to return. Learning to read and write in first grade, he sent Mother the following note: "Grannie, my cat got run over. I am so sad."

She wrote back, "I'm ready to bust out of this house and run all the way to Highway 64, hitchhiking to Texas yelling, '"I'm coming, Zachary! Grannie's coming!"'"

So it was that three-year-old Zachary, who had wanted to pray for Granny and Daddy George to come back home immediately, got his prayer answered by age six. As Granny and Daddy George pulled into our driveway, he and Zeke and two-year-old Rachel held up the welcome home banner. I, heavy with child, waddled into Mother's arms with a sense of deep gratitude and relief, and made her an offer she couldn't resist.

"Wanna go out to lunch and split a spinach salad?"

There is a time for everything,
and a season for every activity under heaven:
a time to be born and a time to die,
a time to plant and a time to uproot.
ECCLESIASTES 3:1-2

Fried Worms, Anyone?

Gabe, our grand finale, was just one year old when the recession of the eighties caused his daddy's construction business to evaporate before our very eyes. I had always envisioned that I would have the privilege of being a full-time wife and mother like my own mother had been. If I had been raising a family during the sixties as she had, perhaps it might have worked out that way. But I entered upon my career as a wife and mother in the inflationary seventies and eighties, and like so many other couples, my husband and I discovered that two incomes were now essential to provide even a minimum standard of living for our family of six.

His new job managing a private lake with a social club meant we would have a modest home provided for us on the lake, which was a dream come true for our boys. Unfortunately, it also required that someone cook for the clubhouse socials. You can guess who that someone was.

Thankfully, the children could often accompany me and were sometimes even a big help in the kitchen. I did very well generally, which is one more reason why I never doubt the existence of God, but I do remember preparing for an elegant candlelight dinner and actually misplacing a pan of marinating pork chops. I frantically searched the kitchen with no luck and finally realized guests were arriving for their pre-dinner socializing. Providentially, I had enough individual servings of prime rib in the freezer that I could go straight to Plan B. Just as I began to prepare the prime rib, I heard a female voice that resembled the quality and volume of a pipe organ behind me.

"Becky, Dahling, you *do* create the most interesting centerpieces!" I followed her soprano laugh to the dining room, where, in the middle of the romantic candles and cascading floral arrangement, sat a plastic industrial dishpan full of raw red pork chops aesthetically floating in teriyaki marinade. It looked more like I was hostessing a hog-killing than an elegant buffet. Noting the chairman of the social committee in her basic black with pearls trying gallantly to sound amused while nauseated, my faith was strengthened, not only in God, but in womankind. I discreetly transported the giant tub to the kitchen while muttering to myself, "Nothing like raw unidentifiable animal parts floating in a dishpan to whet appetites, I always say."

That was the worst that ever happened, but there were many near misses of which my clientele remained blissfully unaware. The kids love to tell about my famous wild rice. I, for one, think that weevils definitely resemble coarse ground black pepper when mixed with exotic grains of cooked rice. So, apparently, did my dinner guests. All except one man who made a neat pile of them in the corner of his empty plate. I thought it was pretty rude of him, too, when everyone else ate their weevils as polite dinner guests should. Zach added insult to injury by referring to my dish as Mom's Famous Wild Life Rice.

And of course there was the luncheon where Gabriel investigated a lettuce leaf slowly crawling off the salad bar and found a fat green worm at play. Not the sort of thing we could expect Gabe to keep under his hat, now could we?

After some time, and for no obvious reason, I began to have the feeling that I had better get out of catering while the getting was good. I examined all my abilities and assets, and realized that my resumé consisted almost entirely of an uncanny ability to attract creeping, crawling things. I even considered a possible market for fried worms. After all, in some countries people enjoy chocolate dipped ants, and in Texas, some people eat rattle snakes, though I do believe they cook them first.

My desire had been to go back to college when Gabe started kindergarten, but when faced with the possibility of a lifetime in catering, Scott and I began to seriously discuss the feasibility of my starting back to school as soon as possible. We decided it really would be in the best interest of humanity and the animal kingdom to get me out of food service entirely, though we had no idea how we could swing it. By the grace of God, Scott found a different job which did not require that his wife cook, and we began to look for another place to live.

I am fully convinced
that no food is unclean in itself.
ROMANS 14:14
෨

The Worm Farm

"Come on in!" I flung the door of our new home wide to admit Mary, my friend who had cheerfully dedicated almost a week of her busy life to helping me look for a house in our price range. Miraculously, we had actually found one.

"Be careful of that little electrical wire hanging over your head there," I said as I took her hand to guide her past the tools heaped in the middle of the floor of the new home we had actually bought—a thirty-year-old, 850-square-foot cabin on a huge wooded lot on the banks of the exclusive private lake where we had previously been employed.

I could almost see Mary's logical mind re-counting the six members of our family and the one bedroom in the cabin. She looked as if her knees might buckle.

"Oh, Mary," I tried to reassure her, "We just couldn't uproot the kids, especially the boys. After living in the country, we'd go bonkers living in town. So there's only one bedroom for the time being. We'll stack the kids to the ceiling in bunks and Scott and I can sleep on the couch in the living area—just for the time being. Look at that view!" I desperately tried to communicate my vision of "what was to be."

"Did you ever see such a gorgeous lake? And right out our picture window! Look at the size of those cypress trees! Running water? Well, of *course* we have running water, silly!" To myself I said, "*hot* water will come later."

"A bathtub? Not yet, but that tin box-looking thing in the corner is a shower…sort of. Did I mention the view? I did, huh?"

"Smell? Oh, that. Scott's working on the septic system." The expression on Mary's face could only be described as one of shock, and I detected a fading in my own rose-colored glasses. "Look at that spectacular bluejay!" I ventured. "Noise? Oh, the barking! Daisy finally had her puppies. Just eleven."

Mary clutched her adam's apple and this time her knees actually did buckle. Even with the shock of seeing the cabin for the first time, it seemed to me she was taking the news about Daisy's pups awfully seriously, but then I realized the source of her pain.

"Oh my goodness! I forgot to tell you to duck! We're hanging our clothes on that piece of rope 'til Scott gets a closet built." And so went the tour until the brilliant orange sun settled into the coolness of the lake in front of us with an almost audible sigh. A gorgeous display, but even that brought its own set of problems.

"Yes, it *is* getting dark in here," I admitted. "No overhead lighting yet, but it can be so cozy sitting around the glow of a fireplace in the dark, don't you think?" *Oh gosh! I'm beginning to sound like Pollyanna on amphetamines. I've got to get her out of here!* I gently took Mary by the arm to avoid shocking her further, possibly into catatonia.

"Let's go down to the lake and watch the sunset!"

I wish I could say that I felt as optimistic as I had tried to sound about our decision to live in the old cabin and renovate as we could afford the time and money. Our family of six had reached its maximum number, but it was rapidly increasing in sheer volume. Scott, my give-me-wide-open-spaces husband, is six feet tall with shoulders that strain his new business suit. Zach and Zeke were ten and nine and showing every promise of being at least as big as their Dad. Rachel was a petite six and Gabriel, three. It looked to be a long winter.

The hardest thing I remember about the winter of '89 was the tin, box-looking thing called a shower. It was inevitable that we would have trouble with each other. Under the best of circumstances, I do not like a shower. It is impossible to shave one's legs in any sort of lady-like posture while standing. However, the shower did not like me, either. All the other members of the family could bathe in the thing without any great problem, but almost as soon as I turned on the spigot, the drain would stop up and water would begin to flow out onto the bathroom floor. This did not happen to anyone else in the family.

I finally developed a technique which involved turning on the spigot for only a few seconds at a time, and so managed to survive the first weeks of winter taking showers while my heart longed for a long soak in a hot tub with a good book. I even attempted to re-create the feeling by sitting close to the furnace with my feet in a pan of hot water. Definitely not the same.

Scott was determined to solve the mystery of why the shower overflowed only when *I* was in it. He decided to observe my routine. I entered the shower, hit the spigot, got halfway through my scrub down, and sure 'nuff, water began to lap up and over the edge of the tin box. I heard Scott muttering. Poking his head through the curtain, he peered at my feet incredulously.

"Becky," he asked, "You're not standing on the drain, are you?"

When the arctic winds began to blow across the East Texas lake, I had moments when I felt it might have been wiser to have taken our chances on going bonkers in the city, and I thanked God for my El Salvador experience.

Whatever my doubts were, I had to keep up a good front because my claustrophobic husband was about to go crazy. During the winter months, he mostly just came home from work and curled up in a fetal position, biting his fingernails while his eyes darted back and forth with a look of caged terror. The children didn't seem to mind the close quarters as they jumped, wrestled, and crawled over him.

On his better days, he would uncurl himself and do a bit of remodeling. Gabriel, too young to appreciate "what was to be," found this upheaval to be very unsettling. Finally, as he surveyed yet another wall his Daddy had demolished, he gathered his coat in hand.

"I'm ready to go home now," he announced.

"Gabe, this *is* home…remember? We have a lake and everything! Just look at the view!"

He was not to be consoled. "But this house is broken!" he wailed.

When spring sprang, however, the whole family changed its tune. Gabriel discovered the incredible world of frogs, not to mention chameleons, snakes, and skunks—a veritable worm farm. Zach and Zeke spent their days exploring the woods and fishing for crappie. Rachel became a waterbug and begged to swim every day. Scott began to heal through nature therapy: bird watching. He would arise early on weekends and, with a cup of coffee and his binoculars, settle into his recliner and watch the birds in quiet fascination.

By spring, my dream too, had come true. I had a real bathtub—almost better than the view, even with the dogwood in bloom. And with the cabin almost inhabitable, we could begin to turn our thoughts toward another dream—getting Mom through college.

O Sovereign Lord, you are God!
Your words are trustworthy,
and you have promised these good things to your servant.
Now be pleased to bless the house of your servant...
and with your blessing
the house of your servant will be blessed forever.
2 SAMUEL 7:28-29

THIRTEEN

Awkworm Situations

Have you ever had one of those experiences when you wish you could just disappear? Often I want to do that, especially when I find myself in a situation where it is rude, sacrilegious, or unthinkable to do what I have an uncontrollable urge to do—laugh. Scott has been so embarrassed by my outbursts in the past that he is now skittish about sitting next to me in any formal situation. It's an awful affliction, and I honestly don't know what to do about it.

It's pure agony to try to suppress the laughter. I bite into the flesh of my cheeks, cover my mouth and nose, and still…I somehow manage to blow. I once got tickled at a prayer meeting—not a light-hearted women's prayer meeting, but a serious, down-on-your-knees, prayer meeting in Glen Eyrie, Colorado. A nice young fellow was leading us in prayer, and I know this is no excuse, but he had the most nasal tone I have ever heard from the mouth of a human being.

On top of "the voice" came a string of requests addressed to the Almighty with an incredible preponderance of "eths." "Dear Father, blesseth Thoueth the meetingeth hereeth in our presenceth." The giggle bubbled up from the belly, threatening to pour forth through my mouth and nose. I slapped my mouth and held my nose. The sound I issued resembled a suckling pig. My shoulders began to shake, and I could sense Scott's presence seething next to me. Then, there was a blessed pause, and I thought I might be saved. But no. "Andeth ifeth it pleaseth Thine heart, maketh useth..." At that point I began to wheeze. There was to be no mercy. It waseth the prayer that hadeth no endeth.

Finally, I grabbed a Kleenex™, feigned being overcome with emotion, and ran out the door pretending to sob. Actually, by the time I got out of there, I was laughing so hard I did began to weep. After the service, Scott was livid with shame and embarrassment. I apologized profusely, but then I noticed how Scott's nostrils flared when he got mad and how his ears twitched when his voice got loud, and I found myself once again in a situation where fools laugh and angels fear to tread.

Everyone I'm sure has had the experience of going into the wrong restroom a time or two. Granted, there are some of us who have done this a bit more often than others, but my mild-mannered, deeply spiritual father has the prize for the most embarrassing example of this awkward situation. The horrible part is that he was stuck in the women's restroom at no less than the prestigious Dallas Theological Seminary where he was taking a layman's course. He came to realize that something was awry when he saw a woman's purse drop down in the stall next to him. All he could think of was how he would explain his presence to Dr. Howard Hendricks if he should come strolling down the hallway just as Daddy ran in panic out of the ladies' room.

Of all of the awkward places to laugh, funerals must certainly top the list. I'm sure even the most godly of ministers have had funny situations occur at that delicate time. Perhaps a bit of laughter is a good thing at some funerals, particularly when a person has lived a full life, to a ripe old age, for the Lord. Then the service takes on an almost festive feeling, a celebration of joy at the beloved's homegoing. It would have been nice if that had been the reason for the laughter of Jamie, my willowy blond blue-eyed cousin who is my opposite in looks but my clone in nature.

Jamie went alone to the funeral of a friend of hers, a young man she had known in high school. She arrived early, taking a seat near the front of the chapel in the funeral parlor. Just seeing the coffin brought a wave of emotion, and she dabbed at her eyes with a tissue. People began filing in until the chapel was almost full.

Mmm, Jamie thought to herself, *I don't recognize any of Jeff's friends here. Well, it's been a few years since I've seen Jeff. Friends change with time.*

After an opening hymn, the minister ascended the pulpit and began the eulogy. "We are gathered here today to honor the memory of Mr. Samuel K. Whitzle…"

Mr. Who-zle? Jamie thought, *Oh, my goodness sakes alive! I'm at the wrong funeral. I am sitting here grieving for a person I have never had the privilege of meeting. And Mrs. Whitzle must wonder why a tall blond girl on the front row is grieving for her husband. I've got to find a way to get out of here.* In the end, Jamie used the old "overcome with emotion so I have to leave" ploy, covering her convulsions with her damp tissue as she left out the back door.

Shortly thereafter, we put our heads together during a visit and exchanged ways to back out of a variety of tight spots. Jamie owes me for the sobbing technique, but I owe her for helping me to perfect the stalling procedure that has saved my life a time or two. She developed it one day at a swimming pool with her beautiful little girl. A woman came up, complimented her child, and asked what her name was.

"Well, I drew a blank," Jamie described the situation, "How could I tell a stranger I suddenly could not remember the name of my own child? So I stalled, 'You mean that little girl in the green bathing suit? The one with the big blue eyes? The one calling me Mommy?' Finally," she finished, "I remembered my own daughter's name."

Thanks to Jamie's expertise, I have often used the stalling technique myself. It comes in quite handy when I make a phone call and cannot remember who it is that I have dialed. I'll say, "Well, hi! This is Becky Freeman. Do you remember me? (*Oh, how I wish I remembered you.*) Well, how in the world have you been and what have you been up to?" Usually there are enough clues in their answer that it will eventually dawn on me to whom I am speaking. It's a little awkward if you've dialed, say, the electric company, and the woman on the other end is trying to figure out why you are acting so folksy during a business transaction.

Sometimes there are entire days that come under the topic of Awkworms. One such day occurred in early fall, the first time I had planned to go to a Women's Bible Study at our church. For starters, I went out to my car and the door handle fell off in my hand. I went around, climbed through the passenger's side to the driver's seat, and managed to finally get it to start. Then the engine began to make noises that reminded me of the sound my clothes dryer made when one of my children had poured an entire bag of dog food into the tumbler. Seconds later, the car began to hiss and spurt and foam and spout. I started to ignore it, but I hated to humiliate myself by driving it down the road. I gave up and ran inside to call my friend Janna and asked her if I could hitch a ride.

"Sure, " she said, "But I have to be there early so I'll pick you up in five minutes." No problem. All I had left to do was change shoes and I'd be ready. As I reached for my shoe in the murky depths of my closet, I stubbed my toe on a cold, hard object. Taking quick revenge, I gave the thing another hearty kick and found I had just knocked over an entire gallon of white paint in the floor of my closet. I hurriedly threw an old towel over the spreading paint so I could think about what I should do next.

At that moment I heard Janna's car honking in the driveway. I took another look at the impossible mess and made my decision. *Oh, well,* I thought, *out of sight, out of mind I always say. With that towel over everything, it doesn't look that bad.* I grabbed my shoes and ran to Janna's car, slipping on my shoes as I ran. I started to tell Janna what a hectic morning I had had when she looked at my feet in horror. Little did I know that I had stepped in the paint with my hose-covered foot.

"What's that?" she asked, grimacing. When I glanced down I saw globs of white paint oozing over the top of my shoe.

We elected to go on to church where I dashed to the ladies' room. I washed off the paint to the best of my ability, but even that left visible portions of my foot with albino splotches. After Bible study, another friend, Susan, offered to take me home.

"I'd *love* to see your house—where you write—how you manage." I could feel the panic start to rise as I remembered what my house looked like when I had run out the door that morning. However, I needed the ride and it was too late to back out. Susan would just have to accept my house the way it was.

Once we arrived at my front door stop, I warned Susan that things might be a little messy. First we encountered the trail of white painted footprints leading from the front door to the closet.

"That's an interesting touch," Susan commented. Once in the kitchen, I cleared the counter of cereal bowls and warm, sticky milk and opened the refrigerator to see what I might offer Susan in the way of a snack. I have encountered many interesting things in my fridge, but this time, even I was shocked. Staring me in the face was the dead carcass of a rabbit and the pelt of a squirrel. It was not a sick prank, I realized. Zach and Zeke were big game hunters these days. I quickly slammed the refrigerator door and thought, *I can't let her see in there. She and Bill are so well-to-do. She'll think I'm related to Jed Clampit.* Turning, I noticed Susan staring at my calendar.

"Becky," she quizzed, "It's September and your calendar is still on May."

"I know, Susan," I answered, "I just like to pretend its Spring." *Like everyone keeps up with what month it is,* I thought to myself.

"Well, let me see where you work!" she said cheerily, waiting to be impressed. There was nothing I could do but show her the desk which I currently shared with Gabriel. There sat my computer next to a large ceramic piggy bank. A stack of files was graced with the remains of a peanut butter and jelly sandwich. Susan never batted an eyelash, bless her. Thankfully, I have landed in a group of people at my church who take me just as I am, without one plea.

Especially do I love and appreciate my pastor, Ralph Anderson, and his wife, Joyce. When I think about Ralph I think of the days when I catered Wednesday night meals before the evening service. My helper was Lisa, a mentally handicapped but loving little go-getter of a girl. Every Wednesday at 11:00 A.M., Lisa and Ralph participated in a little ritual that was lovely to see. Lisa had permission to buzz Ralph's study from the kitchen, and before long Ralph would show up with a deck of Uno™ cards and delight Lisa by playing several rounds with her in the dining hall. The loser always bought the winner a coke.

As I watched that scene, time and again—Ralph and Lisa laughing and playing together as the sun streamed in from the skylight above—it never ceased to touch my heart. To me, a great pastor is not necessarily an accomplished speaker or a superior leader, although Ralph has those qualities. Great is the man who quietly talks and listens to children in the halls and takes the time to show friends like Lisa that he cares. That's Ralph.

I called Ralph yesterday to ask him if he and Joyce had ever experienced an awkward moment in their years of ministry. He related something that occurred in the early years of their time at our Aldersgate Church, around 1970. When Ralph and Joyce took the pastorate, the church was very young. It had split from a Methodist church in town, and there was concern as to whether the newly established evangelical church would even survive. The first pastor stayed for only five months. To the relief of the congregation, Ralph and Joyce arrived and soon added a sense of warmth and stability to the growing church.

One night, about a year later, Ralph and Joyce awoke to the sound of glass breaking accompanied by flashes of light and searing heat coming from the industrial cleaning company next door. They soon realized a roaring fire was engulfing the building, so they bundled up their two-year-old Lisa, taking her outside to safety. They were worried that the fire might traumatize her, but their fears were obviously groundless. They watched their small daughter clap her hands with glee and belt out a rousing chorus of "Happy Birthday to Me" to the dancing firelight.

Ralph swung into action and sent Joyce to the house of Ham and Nancy Kate Hamilton, one of the founders of the church, to seek shelter and bring help. Somewhere around 12:30 A.M., Ham was awakened by an insistent knock at the door. Ham was a little hard of hearing, so it was remarkable that he woke up at all. Still in his shorts, he went to the door and heard the voice of the young pastor's wife.

Peeking out the window he saw Joyce carrying her child, frantically yelling, "Ham! We've had a fire! We've had a fire!" Ham shook his head in disbelief, ran back to the bedroom to grab his pants and wake up his wife.

"Nancy Kate! Get up! The pastor's wife and baby are out there on the front porch, and I don't know what to do."

Nancy Kate scolded, "Ham, what's the matter with you? Let her in!"

"I'm sorry, Nancy Kate, but I didn't know what to say. Just when we thought we'd found a quiet, loving couple that might stay awhile, the pastor's wife is out on our frontyard and is yelling that they've gone and had a fight."

When Ham and Nancy Kate finally let Joyce come in and discovered she had been yelling about a fire, not a fight, relief spread across both their faces, much to Joyce's puzzlement. It was years before Ralph and Joyce discovered the midnight panic that Ham's hearing impaired ears had caused, and ever since it's become one of the famous "tell-it-again" stories around campfires and retreats.

Actually, awkward situations can make for fairly tasty worms in life's cup of tea. You just have to know how to serve them. You've got to let them set out to dry awhile. After some time has passed, re-hydrate the awkworms by re-telling the story. Mmmm, delicious. Much more appetizing with time and a few garnishes on the side. By sharing your experiences, awkward situations become less threatening and unbearable. It's comforting to know that each of us will have the opportunity to deal with our own share of awkworms.

He remembered that they were but flesh.

PSALM 78:39

ॐ

The Worm Turns

Once we had determined I would go back to college to finish my degree, the next question became, "What did I want to be other than a mom?" What were my talents other than cooking for a crowd? Like a good mother, I discussed it with the children, and one evening around the dinner table we went on to discuss toward what heights *they* might be aspiring.

Zach wavered between being a priest or a ballerina, which I thought was interesting since we are neither Catholic nor coordinated.

Zeke's answer took me somewhat aback, given his gentle nature. "An enemy," he responded firmly. (Hey—it'll sure save on those pesky college tuition bills.)

Turning to Rachel, I posed the question in a neutral-gendered, designed-to-encourage-nonstereotypical-thinking manner: "Would you like to be a doctor or a nurse when you grow up?" After much thought, she replied in true feminist form.

"I'll have to wait and see which outfit looks better on me."

I'm beginning to feel I'm failing somewhere in this area because when I asked Zach the question, "Why do we treat women with respect?" he answered sincerely, "Because you never know when you might need to use one."

Having drawn a blank in my quest for a career direction, I agreed to teach VBS that summer, which I have since learned can often stand for Very Bad Situation. One morning, I happened to stroll by the church kitchen with a preschooler named James by the hand. The aroma of fresh baked goods deliciously perfumed the air, and seeking to make conversation with James, I remarked, "Mmmmm…what is that wonderful smell?"

James obviously possessed an esteem for his small self that needed no boosting. "It's me!" he beamed.

I loved it, and of course all the other moms loved it when I reported it to them, and that night, inspired by James, I sat down with my dog-eared journal and chuckled over the long list of questions I'd been asked at different times by my own or by other people's children.

"Mom, how do they make snakes turn into rubber?"

"What are those minnows that come in a can and that people eat?"

"Why does my finger gots two elbows?"

"Is your lap just for babies tonight?" (An excellent postpartum guilt inducer!)

"How do they squeeze people into those tiny airplanes up in the sky?"

"Are you potty-trained, Mom?"

"Can I have ice cream with chocolate chipmunks?"

"Will you put this up, Mom? I'm afraid I'm about to get into it."

"Why don't you just buy that zucchini swimsuit and let's get out of this lady store?" (Because I would need enough material to make a tent for the entire Saudi desert in order to cover up the stretch marks you gave me five years ago, thank you.)

Last but not least, as Gabe observed his first caterpillar, "What is that worm doing with a sweater on?"

I laughed that night, but realized there were tears on my face. "Wait a minute!" my heart cried. "I *need* these little critters in my life! I'm not ready to give this up!"

And so my decision to become a kindergarten teacher was partly selfish. My last baby was standing at Kindergarten's door. As a kindergarten teacher I would be relieved of the pressure of pleasing adults with discriminating tastes, and I could teach kindergartners who *love* messy food and bugs and worms.

Actually, I had always been somewhat of an educator at heart. I recall when Zeke was a baby. For a long period of time everything in his infant world was a "bean-bean." I dutifully sought to introduce him to new vocabulary, particularly days when I had him pinned in his highchair for lunch.

"Zekey," I said to my noodled, highchaired student. "This is spaghetti. Can you say spaghetti?"

He blinked two Ragu-covered eyelashes and replied in absolutely perfect English, "Spa-bean-bean!"

While we're on the subject of Zeke, I know that you have been waiting breathlessly for the chapter dealing with, "Raising the Difficult Child," or "How To Contain Your Little Wormonger." Actually, I feel uniquely qualified to discuss the problem of "Dealing with the Perfect Child," which Zeke just about is.

He did not begin life that way. He was born just eighteen months after Zach and got off to a terrible start. He had colic and cried for hours at night, even though I breast fed him and rocked him and did all the right mother-things I knew to do. I did find some comfort in a book by Anne Ortlund, *Your Children Are Wet Cement*. My mother spotted the book on the kitchen table one evening as she walked the floor with screaming Zeke.

"Are you sure that's not, *Put Your Children in Wet Cement?*" she inquired.

As Zeke became a toddler, he was like a spider monkey, able to shinny up my legs and into my arms, clinging to my neck twenty-four hours a day, seven days a week it seemed, screaming most of the time.

Finally one morning Mother called when I was at wit's end, drowning in a sea of tears and wondering if I would ever be able to enjoy this unhappy baby. I began to wail out my misgivings and then noticed the other end of the line was very quiet, which to say the least, was unusual.

"Becky," she began, and I seemed to hear something akin to awe in her voice, "something happened this morning as I was praying for you and Zekey Baby that doesn't happen to me very often. It was as if the Lord shot a message into my head. It was very clear. It was, Zeke will be Becky's blessing."

Needless to say, I took heart, and have lived to see that prophecy more than fulfilled. This is the child who received the "Most Tenderhearted" award three times in a row in school. The little guy inherited bad teeth and suffered too much for his age in the dentist's chair, yet when he overheard me complain about the high dental bills, he told me earnestly, "I'll ask the dentist not to give me a prize next time so he won't charge you so much."

Zeke loves to work alongside his Dad, has patience beyond his years with other family members, and usually gives in to their desires. He will ride happily in the car for hours, and his favorite hobby is *reading!*

I had actually begun to worry about him until I overheard a conversation between him and his older brother and younger sister. Gabe was napping and the older three were sitting around a picnic table on the back porch enjoying the breeze from the lake. I was enjoying the fact that they were all sitting. They were growing so fast, it gave me a chance to look them over carefully and see what time was doing. Where had my babies gone?

Zach was so obviously an Arnold—stocky, deeply tanned, straight dark brown hair, dark dancing eyes. Zeke, a total opposite, was so obviously a Freeman—lanky, with light brown hair, tender brown eyes, quiet and soft spoken. And Rachel Praise?—light brown curls, freckled, with an upturned nose, fair skin…What long recessant gene pool had she drawn from to be another totally different child? Whichever it was, Gabe had dipped from the same pool for his fair skin and freckles, but checked in at the Arnold's Spanish stream for his almost black hair. But it looks like his build is going to be the best from the Freeman pool, long and lean with broad shoulders.

In my meditative state, I smiled as I thought of how relieved Mother must be with the physical makeup of her grandchildren.

Years back, when she had realized Scott and I were headed for the altar, she had worried about our progeny. "Becky dear," she had asked, "what if your children inherit the Arnold legs and the Freeman arms?"

I had to admit—if the unthinkable happened, we might produce a line of humans with the posture of a gorilla, but we were so in love we were willing to risk it. There on the deck that gorgeous day I knew our worries had been groundless. They were all fine looking specimens. I was delighted with them, and with the moment.

I hadn't been paying much attention to their conversation, but Zach made a pronouncement that caught my ear.

"I'm special because I'm the oldest," he said with pride.

Rachel quickly countered, "But I'm Daddy's sweetheart because I'm the only girl." Both turned to Zeke who thought for a moment, grinned, and assumed a saint-like expression.

"Yes, but *I'm* perfect," he intoned.

No one raised a voice to contradict him.

He is the Rock,
his works are perfect and all his ways are just.
DEUTERONOMY 32:4

Worms in My Mother's Coffee

Perhaps the time has come to talk about my mother, the kind of mother who would suggest you "put your children in wet cement." Obviously, she's not your average, run-of-the-mill old mother, but then, whose mother is? She tries hard to avoid becoming set in her ways, but I've noticed a number of things lately that have caused me to suspect that she is, well...shall we say, resistant to change? Months and months after a new style of clothing is in vogue, she finally notices, complains, issues a proclamation about its foolishness, and ends up buying it just before it goes out of style.

When sweat pants swept the nation, I sat with her one day at the cafeteria munching our spinach salads and gazing absently out the window. We were watching people in the parking lot, and when I glanced at Mother she seemed a little glum.

"I think it's sad," she said with an air of resignation.

"Sad? What's sad?" I inquired.

"The whole world is running around in their pajamas. Nobody ever gets dressed anymore."

I did my best to console her. "Sorry, Mother, but I think change is here to stay."

With a sigh, she gathered her packages, and we began our stroll back down the length of the mall.

A couple of years later she had to come to terms with stirrup pants. She now owns two pair, but she is still prone to philosophize. "Have you noticed," she observed, "that we now have a large percentage of women who goose step through the mall because their stirrup pants are too short?"

I made the mistake of giggling, and she felt encouraged.

"Something else I've noticed that I think is interesting. We all feel so comfy in the overgrown tops that go with the stirrup pants. We think because our posteriors are covered up, we don't have to worry about them. But when we put on a big sweater which also happens to cup in just under the bottom line, so to speak, we might as well pin a bright red bow on our backside!"

I had to laugh, even as I tugged at the bright red sweater topping my stirrup pants. "Oh, well," I offered, "It's possible that stirrup pants may virtually eliminate fallen arches and flat feet in a generation of women."

While my mother is prone to philosophize and is also an honor graduate of her high school class, this does not necessarily mean that she is a left brained, detailed individual. After all, I did not spring forth on this earth out of nothing, so right brained that I tilt in that direction when I walk. As you might expect, this almost overpowering genetic tendency has programmed both of us to look for the fun things in life and to avoid all machinery more complicated than an electric can opener.

Mother is constantly amazed by people who love gadgets and rush out to buy the newest as soon as they are available. We bought her her first microwave oven, and to her great credit, she overcame her fear of being vaporized and now wonders how she ever managed without it.

But Mother is also very aware that a refusal to learn new skills is a sign of aging, and as we have seen, she does not intend to *age*. She remembers that Grandmother Arnold never consented to use the new dishwasher in her apartment. She also remembers buying a tape player for Nonnie and how delighted Nonnie seemed to be when she opened her gift. Some years later Mother found the tape player still in the box on a top shelf in Nonnie's closet. It had obviously never seen the light of day. Consequently, she *will* eventually learn to operate the latest, absolutely necessary advance in technology. Take her new "under the counter" coffee maker for an example.

Mother used the standard American coffee pot for most of her life. She put water in the pot, put coffee in the basket, put the lid on the basket, and then plugged the cord into an electrical outlet. The pot made happy, gurgling noises while she leaned against the counter humming and tapping her fingers on the counter in anticipation. This was a comforting and satisfying morning ritual for many years, and she found no fault with it until she visited her brother-in-law and found that *he* had a new coffee pot which, when set the night before, had *his* coffee waiting for him the moment he staggered into the kitchen. He was able to have a cup even *before* his eyes were open. Could it possibly be that it was time to retire her faithful percolator, even though it was in perfect working order?

Mother decided to purchase an "under the counter" coffee maker, and I mention this only because such a coffee maker requires slightly more know-how and attention to detail than the average modern coffee maker, and certainly more than Mother's fifteen-year-old eight-cup percolator with the dark brown interior. The new coffee maker was familiar in that the operator first filled the pot with water. But the similarities ended there. In the older version the water remained in the pot. In the new version, the water had to be poured from the pot into the stand and the empty pot placed under the drip spout, where the pot (if everything has been done right) received the coffee.

The night she brought the new contraption home, Mother carefully prepared the coffee maker as directed and went to bed with visions of fresh-brewed coffee awaiting her at 6:00 A.M. The next morning, much to her dismay, she found the coffee maker silent and cold, the pot empty—just as she had left it the night before. She tried again the next night, only to awaken to the same disappointment. She decided at this point that the automatic device must be defective and was about to bundle the coffee maker up and return it to the department store. Then Daddy read the directions carefully, discovering that it was not only necessary to set the automatic turn-on for 6:00, but that it had to be set for 6:00 A.M.

And so, on the third morning after her purchase, Mother awoke to the aroma of coffee wafting down the hallway from the kitchen to her bedroom, and she congratulated herself on conquering yet another technological advance. Before long, setting up the coffee pot at bedtime became routine.

About three months after becoming accustomed to having fresh coffee almost before her eyes were open, Mother shuffled down the hall to the kitchen to find the coffee freshly made—on the kitchen counter, the kitchen floor, and a few inches into the den carpet. She had poured the water into the coffee maker stand the night before, set the pot down on the counter, and gone to bed. The next morning, the coffee maker did its thing, but there was no pot under the drip spout to catch the lovely brew.

This has happened often enough over the last two years that the varnish has come off the cabinet where the coffee runs down on its way to the den carpet. On other mornings, she has arisen to find the coffee pot sitting under the drip spout, dry and hot as a pistol—she had forgotten to put the water in. Other variations have included finding the pot full of hot water, signaling that she had failed to put coffee in the stand, and finding it too weak to wake anybody up because she had not only remembered to put the water in the stand, she had put it in twice.

She continues to get the coffee ready to perk at bedtime but has given up on setting the pot on "automatic" anymore, feeling it just can't be trusted. Recently, however, Daddy observed her sleepily pouring the water intended for the vaporizer into the coffee pot stand.

When Mother began to talk about purchasing a 160-horse-power fruit and vegetable juicer, you can imagine the wave of excitement that swept through friends and family. She had become interested in this gadget (against all her right brain programming) because it was advertised on TV by a muscle-bound gentleman in his late seventies. I suspect she took a sidelong glance at Daddy snoring in his easy chair, compared him to the gentleman on TV, and decided to have a shot at adding the juicer to their vitamin/exercise regimen.

When the juicer arrived, she installed it in a place of easy access beside her coffee maker and began the ordeal of learning to use it. Before that was accomplished, she had managed to shoot three cups of carrot pulp into the crack between her stove and refrigerator, and in a later effort, managed to run three cups of carrot juice down the side of the cabinet. Fortunately, it chose to run about the same course as the coffee usually took, thus avoiding another strip of bare wood.

No discussion of Mother's reluctance to change would be complete without mentioning her antipathy for computers, which (who?) she is convinced are not entirely mechanical but may actually be inhabited by beings from another world. Maybe this is why she finds it hard to hang up on a computerized sales phone call.

She first learned to use a computer some years ago when she purchased a Kaypro™ and taught herself to use one of the first word processing packages, treating our delicate ears to her critique of computer inventors who insisted on using five-syllable words like "documentation" when a three-syllable word such as "manual" would have worked better. (In Texas, manual is a two-syllable word.) The term "tutorial" particularly annoyed her, and she never referred to the tutorial in her computer as anything other than "instructions." She learned to use the word processing capability of her Kaypro, but never had the slightest inclination to see what else was in there. She was quite proud of this rather difficult accomplishment and assumed she would never have to learn anything more than she had already learned. Then her Kaypro died, and she learned it had become so obsolete she couldn't find anybody to repair it. She was outraged.

"Why didn't they tell me when I paid two thousand dollars for a machine that it would become an antique in eight years?" Then with a sigh of relief, she purchased a simple, compact word processor for herself, and one for me, and we wrote happily everafter (well, for a couple of years) on these relatively simple gadgets. If we needed to swap material, we never thought of using a modem, we just made a date to meet halfway between her house and mine at Big Burger with a playground for Gabe. Then, writing took a serious turn, and there were more and more deadlines, closer and closer together. Enter modern computers and fax/modems. It adds a whole new dimension to the question, "Do you do Windows™?"

For weeks Mother circled her new computer, watched other people operate it with idiotic grins on their faces, watched her grandchildren glory in it, avoided looking at Daddy's expectant face each evening as he returned from work, asking if she had used it that day. Then came the publisher's call, "We need forty *more* pages by the end of the week." She did what she always does when she has her back to the wall. She came to grips with technology, but if she loves it yet, she's not about to admit it.

The government has been attempting to overhaul the country's medical system, hoping to provide medical care for all citizens. But even before the government has had its shot at the system, Daddy's company, like most other companies, has been looking for ways to cut insurance. Recently Daddy told Mother that, if they were to be reimbursed 100 percent for medical fees, they would have to make some changes. If one of them were to need to be hospitalized, he or she would have to forego the excellent hospital just five minutes from their house, say good-bye to their dearly beloved doctor, and drive twenty minutes to a strange hospital to see a doctor who would also be a stranger to them. She responded with a shout heard almost round the world. After thinking it over, she calmed down. A few days later, she called me to discuss the situation. It took me a while to answer the phone.

"You must have been outside," she greeted.

"Well, no, actually, I couldn't find the phone."

"Pardon me?"

"Our old one kept coming unplugged in the middle of conversations, so Scott marched out last week and bought a new one, a portable one. So now it gets ported all over the house by the kids and an occasional mother. It's not unusual for it to get covered up with first one thing and then another, depending on how long it is between calls."

"Ah, modern conveniences," she said. "How'd you find it?"

"I just followed the sounds under the bedspread, but last week I had to run to the neighbors and ask them to telephone me so I could run back to the house and hear it ringing. Worked great." It hadn't struck me as particularly funny, but she was whooping and relaying the story to Daddy in the background.

My mother—she laughs at all my stories, even the ones that cost her time and money. But she was not to be diverted long from the topic on her mind, changes in their hospitalization insurance. When the steam began to subside, she did what she does so well. She found philosophical comfort.

"It's becoming clear that our generation—your dad's and mine—have had it awfully good. I'm beginning to suspect that our era has been just a blip in time when a comparatively tiny number of people on the face of the earth lived in remarkable prosperity and comfort. (*There's a lot of good Scrabble material in that sentence!*) I guess we've sort of come to expect it as our due. It takes so much more for your generation just to live. I don't know how you do as well as you do. (*Thanks, Mom.*) I hope and pray that the changes we're looking at in the medical system will mean that you and Scott and David and Barb and Rachel and Gilley—and so many others in the country who have not had it as easy as we have—will benefit. If that happens, we can adjust.

"The thing that worries me about government solutions is that they can create some very peculiar situations like the one we faced when Nonnie needed constant care. If we put her in a nursing home, Medicaid would pay all her expenses because she had no money. But there was no government aid to hire help if we kept her at home, even though it would have cost less than to maintain her in a nursing home."

I heard Mother sigh on the other end of the wire, and I knew she was struggling with the memories and the sorrows, and yes, even guilt because Nonnie had spent the last eighteen months of her life in a nursing home.

"So you can see why I have some reservations about government intervention in our medical system." She thought for a minute more and then continued, "By the way. If you have to put me in a nursing home someday, please try to remember what you did with me."

Don't be deceived, my dear brothers.
Every good and perfect gift is from above,
coming down from the Father of the heavenly lights,
who does not change like shifting shadows.
JAMES 1:16–17
❧

SIXTEEN

Like Death Wormed Over

What I gained in sense of purpose, self-esteem, and head knowledge as I once again entered college, I sacrificed in the orderliness and aesthetics of my life and the life of my family in general. Bear in mind that we were a family of six living in an 850-square-foot cabin which we were also in the process of remodeling, doing all the work ourselves. Perhaps I can be forgiven for failing to receive the "Garden of the Month" award even once during my back-to-college years, and for the innumerable events at which I either failed to arrive on time or managed to forget entirely.

I'll never forget my first day back at college after an absence of ten years. I suppose I had secretly hoped I might be mistaken for an eighteen-year-old coed. At the very least, I expected my fellow students to faint when I revealed to them that I was the mother of four children. The actual reaction was more like, "Just four? Any grandkids yet?"

If I seemed elderly to the college kids, they appeared barely pubescent to me. The girls were wearing ponytails and hair ribbons! I might not have passed for Homecoming Queen, but I felt I did look a picture in my sand-colored corduroy skirt, olive jacket, and burnished leather boots. It was an outfit that obviously said, "Back to School! Crisp nip in the air, falling leaves…"

Too bad the Texas weather said, "You gotta be kidding!"

I sweltered through my first class, and, just before I passed out from heatstroke, I decided to take a restroom break. Checking my autumn pallet makeup in the mirror, I was transfixed. The face looking back at me was wearing a mustache. Evidently I had wiped the sweat from my newly-made up brow, then swiped my hand across my upper lip in an agony of thirst.

"Well," I addressed the coed version of Groucho Marx staring at me from the mirror, "I'll bet *that* impressed the professor."

As I mopped up, I lectured myself. "Wipe that silly mustache off your face! You are finally in college. You are a university student. Now go cash your check at the university bookstore and get yourself a big glass of university iced tea and a collegiate salad at the University S.U.B."

I cashed my check (and sheepishly invested in a few rubber-bands and hair ribbons), filled my lunch tray, and poured myself a huge glass of iced tea, grateful for the security of knowing there were probably no surprises waiting for me at the bottom of the glass. The surprise came when I reached for my wallet to pay for my treat and found it empty at the bottom. I had had the money just ten minutes ago, but it was not there. The next surprise came when I found there was no credit to be had in the university cafeteria. I watched as the university lunch ladies took away my tray, then found a quiet corner, sat collegiately down, and cried.

Later that night, Mother called to see how my day went. She seemed to think it was hysterically funny when I told her I had lost my lunch money on my first day of school.

Back on the home front, my memory continued its downward spiral. I became so lax in my responsibilities as tooth fairy that the children were forced to try a variety of techniques to help the old girl out.

One of the children, having despaired of the tooth fairy ever remembering to look under his pillow, tried placing his tooth in a cool cup of water in the middle of the kitchen table where it could not possibly be missed. However, he forgot that Ms. Fairy was nearsighted and that she would also be thirsty at bedtime.

A second toothless child had the bright idea of tying his tooth to a string hanging from the ceiling fan above his parents' bed, thinking perhaps Mom and Dad might have more influence with the important personage they so much wanted to visit them. However, tooth fairy got too warm in the night, and the bicuspid became airborne somewhere in the wee hours of the morning and flew off into never-never land.

The older children began taking their newly shed teeth with them directly to the store where they could whip them out of their pockets while the tooth fairy was nearby with cash in hand. Gabe continued to struggle bravely on, even though he was understandably not quite clear on just how the tooth fairy system was supposed to work.

On a rare day when I had time to make his bed, I lifted his pillow and found, to my surprise (other mothers would probably have felt horror), the tooth-filled jawbone of a long deceased cow.

"Gabriel James!" I bellowed, "what is this filthy thing doing under your pillow?"

I can only describe the grin on his face as cunning.

"How much do you think the tooth fairy will give me for *that*?" he asked.

During this extremely hectic time, my personal appearance also suffered and eventually became a cause for some periods of mild depression, probably for Scott as well. My Nonnie had an expression to describe people who were not looking their very best for some reason or another. She would pronounce that "they looked like death warmed over." On the morning I had promised to chaperon Zeke's field trip at his school, I woke up with a huge red pimple on the end of my not insignificant schnoz. I thought of my grandmother's expression and decided it was incredibly apt.

"Okay," I told myself. "So you woke up with a little pimple. All right, a *huge* pimple. Why do you, a thirty-something woman, feel thirteen-something again? You will not disgrace your son: you'll be the only one who notices it. You are blowing this tiny imperfection in an otherwise flawless face out of all proportion."

Even so, after inspecting 6,737,294 different specimens of amphibia and reptilia at the Museum of Natural Creatures That Make Mothers Queazy (in the company of thirty third graders who often have the same effect), I was not feeling "good about myself," as the support groups say. And that was *before* it began to rain.

At Burger Billions for lunch break, I fell into the soggy line at the counter, jostled about in a sea of starving nine-year-olds. I caught a sympathetic glance from another field trip mom. Hoping for comfort, I confessed, "I just feel so ugly today. My hair is a wet mess..."

A bright-eyed boy named Christopher chimed in, "Yeah, and you've got a great big red mole thing on your nose, too!"

That did it! I knew the time had come when I simply had to find some time for myself. As soon as the field trip ground to its merciful end, I dropped the children off at home with their dad and headed for Mary's house. Mary is good at many things beside finding nice suburban houses. She sells a lovely line of cosmetics; she is a professional hairdresser who works from a shop in her home; and she is my best friend. That day I needed all she had to give.

Heading straight for her work station, I stepped over two toys and one kitten belonging to Mary's children, Michael and Michele, aged nine and six. I dropped into the beauty chair and sighed deeply.

"You know, you're going to think I'm silly, but I've been so self-conscious about this little blemish today."

"Really?" Mary asked in mild surprise. "Why I..." She moved in for a closer look, stepped back, frowned, clicked her tongue. "I don't believe I've ever noticed anything *that* big on your face before."

"Thanks so much," my reply dripped sarcasm. "I didn't mean to offend you with my gross physical deformity. Excuse me while I go to the bathroom to spackle over this volcano on my nose."

In the bathroom, I applied a couple of Band-Aids™ to the problem, tried to see the humor of it and returned sheepishly to Mary's chair. Attracted by the Band-Aids™, Michael and Michele crawled onto the sofa with the kitten in tow and watched as we discussed what might be a really smashing new hairdo to soothe my battered self-esteem.

"Let's try some color this time, Becky," she suggested. "Something like—Plum Brown. It has nice burgundy highlights to accentuate your red...lips," she finished carefully. Then she set to work turning me Plum Brown.

Considering the large size of the yellow gloves she wore, she deftly measured and mixed and stirred.

"Sorry about these big ol' gloves. I had to use kitchen gloves because I'm out of the thin kind." Looking back over my day, it seemed the least of my problems.

At that moment, Kitty decided to make his escape from the sofa and jumped at Mary, attaching himself to her leg with his small but efficient claws. She screamed and planted her dye-smeared gloves into my forehead, leaving three extra large Plum

Brown fingerprints, complete with burgundy highlights. In the aftermath, our eyes held.

"Nice touch," I said.

Mary apologized profusely while she applied the dye to my head, jerking and yanking at my hair with the huge plastic gloves.

"I'm not hurting you, am I?" She was really very kind, and through my tears I assured her that it did not hurt quite so much as natural childbirth. I tried to remember my Lamaze breathing. Things seemed to settle down and I began to relax and wonder just how gorgeous I might be when the labor was over. Then Mary said something I found more unsettling than what had already happened to me that day. "Uh-oh," was what she said.

"What do you mean, uh-oh?"

"Oh, nothing." Silence. More pulling. "Becky—you haven't been losing a lot of hair lately, have you?"

"No," I fought the swelling panic in my chest. "Am I losing hair now?"

"A little," Mary answered in a professional, try-not-to-alarm-the-customer voice.

"How much is a little?"

"Well…no more than you'd lose with chemotherapy."

From the sofa, Michael and Michele collapsed with glee. "We love it when Becky comes over! This kind of stuff never happens to Mom's other customers. Hey, we could give Becky a T-shirt that says, 'No Hair by Mary.'"

When you've come to the end of your rope, these are the kind of kids who would say, "Tie a knot—and put a noose around your neck."

We managed to salvage what was left of my hair, and I left Mary's house Plum Brown and plum tuckered out. As I drove wearily into the driveway of our home, Gabriel ran out to meet me and smiled his sweet three-year-old smile. He put both hands on my cheeks and gazed tenderly into my eyes.

"Mommy," he said, "you're fat."

At the moment, Nonnie's expression, "looking like death warmed over," seemed inadequate; "death wormed over" fit much better.

Sometimes I feel overwhelmed by the differences between me and the gorgeous Barbie doll look-alikes I see on TV and in magazines. The message they send is clear: "You are only wanted and desired if you look like me."

Then I get mad. How dare the media lead us to believe our worth depends on how we look? God is such a comfort to my sagging ego. He looks past my less than perfect body into my soul, which has had a complete make-over by His forgiveness and love.

Besides, I know a secret. Barbie is hollow inside. I know because Gabe takes her head off regularly. Lord, forgive me for sometimes wanting to do the same thing to real women who wear a size six.

Man looks at the outward appearance,
but the Lord looks at the heart.

1 SAMUEL 16:7

Plump, Juicy Worms

I assume by now you know I hate the word *plump*. Only *chubby* is worse. I much prefer "a few pounds overweight," which sounds more like the condition is temporary. Why not "softly curved"? "Nicely rounded"? Or even "voluptuous"?

With each of my four pregnancies also came an enormous appetite. Food never tasted so delicious, and if it weren't for the accumulation of pounds, I would still miss the way a Big Mac™ melts in my mouth when time is measured in trimesters. As a result of this enormous appetite, I gained an average of sixty-five pounds (that is not a misprint) with every pregnancy. Luckily, a nursing infant takes seven hundred calories a day from his lactating mommy, bless him, so I lost all but five or six of the newly acquired pounds. But...4 times 5 equals 20 anyway you tally it up. Since I had a baby permanently attached to me for nourishment for nearly ten years of my adult life, I enjoyed a decade when my weight was fairly easy to manage.

Then I hit the big "3-0." I began to realize I could no longer expect to eat even the sesame seed off a Big Mac™ without it showing up on *my* buns. To make matters worse, just when I needed Mother to blame for my hereditary genes, she hit middle age, went on her health food regimen, bought walking shoes, and trimmed to a svelte 120 pounds where she has remained for some years now. To her credit, she never mentions my weight, nor suggests I go on any of her seaweed diets with her. But every now and then, she puts her foot in her mouth. For instance...

Not long ago I called to tell Mother about a small triumph. I had dashed into our local Christian bookstore, wearing sweat pants (you already know her opinion of sweat pants), old tennis shoes, and a messy hairdo that wasn't on purpose. I knew the sales lady, and she chose this moment to introduce me to all the customers in the store as a "real writer." I appreciated the attention, but it was not the way I had pictured myself looking at my author's debut. I was chuckling about the incident to Mother when she used the P word in reference to Yours Truly.

"Oh, Becky," she comforted, "those people *loved* you! And all the more because you were plump and disheveled!"

I don't remember anything else she said because I was lost in my own thoughts. *So it's come to this. I am plump.*

To make matters worse, Mother called back the next morning, wanting to make amends.

"Becky," she began tenderly, "you got quiet on the phone yesterday. I think I may have put my foot in my mouth again. I want you to know that you're hardly ever disheveled."

Disheveled? I could care *less* about being disheveled! Disheveled is a temporary, fixable condition, whereas *plump* sounds so *permanent.* Somehow I managed to get off the phone without coming through the line with bared fangs, but when I hung up the receiver I stomped my right foot.

"That does it!" I said, and hitching up my sweat pants, I marched to the mall and bought one of those plastic, cross-country skier deelymabobs that "conveniently folds flat to fit under the bed." I opened it, tried it once, folded it flat, and found it did indeed fit conveniently under my bed as advertised. It fit so conveniently it stayed there for weeks. In fact, that was the only convenient thing about it. Finally I realized it wasn't doing me much good under the bed, so I hauled it out and took it back to the store and exchanged it for a lounge chair.

As I searched for a workable way to get back to a size 8, I began reading the articles that suggested losing weight by simply (Ha!) cutting back on fat and walking—the *healthy* way! Have you seen all the wonderful low-fat products on the grocery store shelves these days? Why, there's everything from no-fat chocolate devil's food cookies to baked—not fried—sour cream and onion potato chips.

I ate all these things by the box full and didn't lose a pound. I did discover it is possible to eat enough fat-free marshmallows and angel food cake to completely negate the fat-burning benefits of walking for exercise.

Then I got really desperate. One evening when I was getting dressed to go out with Scott to a ranch style steak house, I discovered I could no longer squeeze into my favorite pair of black jeans. I tried catching the legs in a closed door and pulling on the waist to stretch them, but to no avail. Then I lay with my shoulders on the bed, sucked in my breath, and put my feet up the wall to get gravity on my side. I ended up wearing a big full skirt, and at the steak house later we watched tiny cowgirls in black jeans and boots prance back and forth with their trays of steak and potatoes. There's a saying in Texas among cowgirls that if you can get a dime into the pocket of your jeans, they're too loose, and I figured these cuties didn't have a dime to their name.

Shortly after making the sad discovery that I could no longer wear my black jeans, I did something I never thought I—nor any other self-respecting Christian woman—would do. I went to a complimentary exam to explore the benefits of liposuction. Let me just say, it was a humiliating experience.

When I got into the examining room the nurse asked me to undress and then to don a garment the size of a Kleenex™. This highlight was followed by even more fun. The nurse then took a Polaroid™ picture of my backside. Why didn't I leave then?

The next thing I knew, a dark and, of course, handsome doctor with a flawless physique entered the room. He began prodding and poking and looking back and forth from me to the Polaroid picture, describing what I could expect with lipo-suction. For starters, I could expect pain. Then there would be the bruises from my hips to my knees. Oh, and did he mention I would have to wear a full-length girdle for months? And there was that pesky little problem of folds of loose skin that might persist after the surgery and require additional nips and tucks. When he left the room I couldn't slip into my dress fast enough.

The grand finale took place when the nurse brought in the projected cost of the surgery, beautifully printed on linen paper in an elegant shade of pink. I expect Dr. Richer-Than-You sent his nurse to deliver the news so that he would be out of swinging distance. I don't care if it is written in gold-leaf calligraphy on sheets of fine pink Japanese parchment, four thousand dollars is a lot of money.

During the drive home, I mentally went through what I would report to Scott. By this point, he was like a frightened rabbit when it came to the topic of my weight. There is nothing inoffensive a man can say to his wife who wants to lose a few pounds. If he says, "I love you just the way you are, Sweetheart," she cries, "And just *what* did you mean by that? What's *wrong* with the way I am?" If he tells her to go on a diet and promises he will support her in it, she replies, "If it's that important to you, you don't love *me*. You only care about how I look." If he says, "Hang the diet. It'll just make you cranky," she will accuse, "I wish just this once you'd be *supportive!*"

By the time I pulled into the driveway, I decided I would make it easy for Scott. He was sitting in his easy chair and looked up expectantly when I entered the room. I slammed the door and walked past him, heading for the bedroom.

"Don't say a word and you'll live longer," I advised.

For a while after that humiliating day, I felt a certain amount of peace with who I was and realized how much I was robbing myself of the happiness of my romantic relationship with Scott by obsessing about my weight. I determinedly got rid of the phrases of self-condemnation playing in my head. Once I settled the issue of weight and self-esteem, what did I do? I went to Wal-Mart™ and bought a Deal-A-Meal™ kit. The morning I dealt my first cards into the vinyl carrying case, I also went to a Bible study at my church. I took a seat next to a cute little blond, one of those abnormalities of nature, and before long the subject of dieting came up, as it too often does.

"Have you seen those Deal-A-Meal™ kits at Wal-Mart™ this week?" she marveled. "What kind of people do you suppose buy those things?"

I thought it over a minute before answering, "Really desperate ones?"

I must say, I lost six pounds and, other than the constant grumbling of my stomach, the diet wasn't all that bad. And shortly after beginning the diet, another man entered my life. His name was Richard.

The day I met Richard began like any other day. I had a breakfast date with Mary, and I might just mention that Mary is knock-em-dead gorgeous. When we're together, I always feel like a wallflower. Men seemed to be drawn to Mary like ants to a picnic, and it's not unusual for men who are perfect strangers to introduce themselves to her. I often wondered what that would be like.

On this particular day, I was in a rush as usual. I decided to dash by Get-It-Kwik to pick up a pack of gum, and as I started into the store, I almost bumped into a large man, wearing baggy pants, a red flannel shirt, suspenders, and a grin as big as all outdoors. I merely smiled at him, but he stopped in his tracks, transfixed it seemed. He stared at me shamelessly.

"Ma'am," he said (Texans make two syllables of it), "you shore are purty." He raked his stocking cap off his balding head, and the expression on his face indicated he was probably hearing heavenly music.

"Why, *thank* you," I replied, flustered a little but not displeased. I hardly missed a step as I went on into the store to finish my errand. By the time I dashed back to the car, I had forgotten about it. I popped the key into the ignition and had a little trouble getting it started. Then I heard a tapping on my window. There stood my starry-eyed admirer. At this point I became flustered and not particularly pleased and began praying that my car would start immediately. The man again swept off his hat, held it reverently in his hands, and spoke to me through the window.

"Ma'am, I'd like to introduce myself. My name's Richard."

I smiled but kept the window closed and shouted through it, "It's nice to meet you, Richard!" Thankfully, the engine finally started. I heaved a sigh of relief, waved good-bye to Richard, and drove the two blocks to the restaurant, really giggling now and planning just how I was going to relay this story to Mary. When I arrived, Mary was there, having struck up a conversation with a nice looking man in the breakfast line.

"You're not going to believe what just happened to me," I said, and by now I was really tickled. "I was at Get-It-Kwik just a minute ago, and this guy..."

"Ma'am?" I heard, just slightly behind me and to my left. Hoping I had not heard what I thought I had heard, I turned to be sure. There he was, big as life, hat in hand.

"Well, hello, Richard," I said nervously and introduced him to Mary. I noticed with a bit of ridiculous pride that he hardly noticed Mary. He only had eyes for me.

"Ma'am, I work at the cafe down the street and I shore would love to buy you a cuppa cawfee sometime." Suddenly the restaurant became so quiet you could hear a pin drop. All commerce halted as every patron and employee fixed their eyes on the little drama being played out before them. Before I could break the news to him that I was a thoroughly married woman, he said the following words I will never forget. "I just never met a woman quite like you."

Mary chimed in, "Oh, lots of people say that about Becky!"

Yeah, I thought, *but I don't think they mean it the way he does! I've got to get control of this.*

"Richard," I said as kindly as I possibly could, "I'm married and have four kids, and I really don't think my husband would want me to meet you for coffee. Thanks so *much*, though." The light went out of his eyes, I presume the heavenly music stopped inside him, and his head drooped noticeably. His hat still in his hands, he turned slowly and left the restaurant. But he had left me a gift. I felt like a starlet, a ballerina, the Queen of Sheba. Mind you, Richard and I were just two ships passing in the night, and yet he had concluded in a few seconds of awestruck admiration that he had "never met a woman quite like me."

I may be struggling, I may even be plump (there, I've said it), but God never made another woman quite like me. Thank you, Richard. You may have been an angel in disguise. If I weren't already married to a wonderful guy, you just might have stolen my heart.

A few days later, Mother drove from the city to the country for a visit, bringing with her a copy of the January/February 1994 issue of *Today's Christian Woman,* one of our favorite magazines. On its cover was a big, beautiful blond woman whose very smile invited you to smile back. Mother pulled out a bar stool.

"I want to read you some of this interview with Liz Curtis Higgs," she said. "It's wonderful. This gal has written a book with a great title—*One Size Fits All and Other Fables*. Isn't that good?" she chuckled. "Listen to this," she began to read from the magazine with gusto the words of Ms. Higgs: "'I notice women in my audiences who are a little larger than average. Their facial expressions are downcast and their style of dress less than flattering...I wanted to let these women know they can be happy and healthy *now* instead of feeling as though they have to diet their way to happiness. Too often we postpone joy until we're a size 10. I've been a size 10 and was no more joyful then than I am now at size 22. Basing our happiness on what the scale says only programs us for disaster!...—*Vogue* doesn't give us the right message. Scripture does.'"

Mother laid the magazine down on the counter. "Just for the record, honey," she said, and I thought she might be about to cry, "I think you're one of the prettiest little things I ever laid eyes on. You light up my life."

Thanks, Mom. Thanks, Richard. And—thank *You, Lord.*

I praise you because I am fearfully and wonderfully made;
your works are wonderful,
I know that full well.

PSALM 139:14
∾

The Worm-mobile

I was pleased to note that our children seemed to be growing in faith by leaps and bounds, even among the chaos, and could even seem to be almost pious at times to the casual observer. I might wish they had learned to depend on prayer in some manner other than through their experiences riding as passengers while their mother roared up and down country roads—always late to class—in an ancient and dilapidated Country Squire station wagon which we referred to as "The Titanic."

Recently I realized that these experiences had not been all bad when Scott decided to run an errand in my car, taking Gabriel along. When Scott started the motor, Gabe was aghast.

"Daddy!" he shouted, "you forgot to pray!"

Because the Titanic and I have been through so much together, I begin most trips with a simple but fervent prayer:

"Lord, please let this car start." Once I leave the driveway, I realize I should have prayed more specifically and at greater length.

The Titanic is the ideal vehicle for transporting wet and muddy boys, their fishing poles, and their worms. Considering the usual menagerie loose in its confines, we hardly notice when the worm box tips over. At one point not long ago, I had a box turtle, a blue-tailed lizard, a chameleon, and a skink running loose in my station wagon.

There are three things, however, that cause the Titanic and me to tremble: trees, country mailboxes, and country ditches. The chrome on the Titanic sticks out all over like porcupine quills, but even more pitiful is the haggard condition of the trees in our circle drive. The children like to use these trees for show-and-tell when their friends come to visit.

"See those trees without any bark on 'em?" asks Zach.

"Wow!" responds the visitor. "Beavers?"

"Nope. My mom can't back out of the driveway without skinning a tree."

My husband used to keep a supply of mailboxes in our garage to replace those of our friends and neighbors after I mowed them down trying to back out of their driveways. I once bagged three in a row, a feat of which I am not really proud, but I have become quite artistic at painting house numbers on the boxes we replace.

As for the ditches, a few months after we moved to our cabin, big white guard rails with reflectors were installed in front of every ditch from our house to the highway. Since I was hauled out of five of those ditches in those first months, I assume the neighbors got together for our mutual benefit and voted to erect the railings.

I also have something of a reputation at the drive-in bank. My car always comes to rest with at least one front wheel on the curb of the concrete island. This is not deliberate on my part, but it does permit me the advantage of getting really close to the tube sucker machine.

One of the things that surprises me about banking is how few people—other than myself—actually take the banking tube right on home with them. I am now on a first name basis with most of the tellers at our bank who, when they see me come in the door, merely smile and hold out their hands.

With this kind of reputation, you can imagine the tension that sweeps through our local Get-It-Kwik when I stop by their drive-in store for gasoline. Until recently, the owner and his employees had managed to prevent my driving away with the pump nozzle still nestled in my gas tank by running outside and waving frantically as I started my car. In spite of their best efforts, the day finally came when I pulled away from the pump with the forgotten nozzle in my gas tank. When I felt the tug and heard the pop, I slammed on the brakes and wearily slumped from my car. Numbly I extracted the nozzle and stood staring at the hose writhing in the wind like a beheaded snake. A kindly man at the next pump looked as if he wanted to weep for me.

"You must be having one of those days," he commiserated. If only he knew how many of "those days" I have accumulated.

Believe it or not, I almost repeated the incident a couple of weeks later, but three employees, watching me carefully from inside the store, sprinted outside in record time and saved the day. "Get-It-Kwik" has taken on an entirely new meaning in our town.

All these have been relatively minor incidents which did not really endanger anybody's life or limbs. But there have been several harrowing instances when Scott had to have his car towed and I have been the only one available. He usually turns whiter than the Pillsbury Dough Boy™ at the prospect of sitting atop or inside any vehicle or machine which is in turn attached to any vehicle which I am driving.

Therefore I was surprised and pleased at his renewed trust in me when he asked me to give him a tow on his riding mower about a mile down the road to where he intended to cut a neighbor's grass. After attaching the mower to the Titanic, he mounted it and I carefully began to pull him down the bumpy, oil-topped road.

Things went along very smoothly. It was a lovely day and the wildflowers were just coming into bloom. I was delighted to see how many varieties there were. Before I realized it, my foot settled into a comfortable forty miles per hour position on the accelerator.

When I happened to glance into the rearview mirror, I saw Scott's elbows flapping up and down like an injured bird in takeoff; I saw six inches of daylight between his posterior and the seat of the tractor and his mouth wide open in a silent scream.

Now, I know I shouldn't have laughed, because it's true; I could have killed him. When I finally got control of myself and brought the Titanic to a halt, the look on Scott's face was a study. It reminded me of Charlie Brown's expression when he had once again trusted Lucy to hold the football so that he could practice kicking.

For he will command his angels concerning you
to guard you in all your ways.
PSALM 91:11
ೲ

Early Bird,
You Can Have the Worm!

L et me make one thing perfectly clear. I don't do mornings.
At least, not well. Or consciously. For me a good day begins
somewhere after 10:00 A.M., after a leisurely bath and large doses
of concentrated caffeine.

Before starting back to school, I could get away with getting
out of bed and shuffling around the house in my robe with a
mole-like expression until the school-aged children became
aware of my unintelligible grunts. This was their cue to rise,
dress, and choose an entree from the breakfast menu: plain bread
with peanut butter, bread lightly toasted, or my specialty, whit-
tle-your-own toast. If the third item on the menu was chosen,
I could count on the smoke alarm to call any remaining little
sleepwalkers into action. I did not think it was funny when Scott
began to refer to the smoke alarm as the dinner bell.

On most mornings, Scott would gulp down a cup of coffee, gather the three older children in his car, and race to meet the school bus on his way to work. Gabe and I were often able to wave good-bye from the front porch, close the door, and snuggle back into a warm bed to catch another hour of sleep. Golden days. Simply golden.

Once I added a full schedule of college courses to my life, it became imperative that I become a more active participant in mornings. Unfortunately, my participation seemed to transform mornings that had previously been chaotic into mornings that became near catastrophic. One particular day, a catch-up-on-chores Wednesday sandwiched between my Tuesday/Thursday class days, I vowed to keep a clear head during the morning's activities with an eye to organizing and improving the situation in the future. If I was going to have to do mornings, I would try to do them reasonably well.

As I considered six people getting ready for school and work in one bathroom the size of a gerbil cage, the scene often reminded me of Gabey's worms writhing in the bottom of my tea glass.

Zach has reached the age when he has discovered he can make an "Elvis Wave" with his bangs, given access to the blow dryer and mirror for a mere thirty minutes.

Rachel Praise has learned that if she stands pressed between the sink and her Daddy as he shaves, she can brush her teeth—if she is careful to dodge his foamy drippings.

Zeke usually makes a few feeble attempts to dash in and find a place at the sink before muttering, "If I can just get my toothbrush, I'll brush my teeth in the kitchen."

Since Gabe is not too far removed from his potty training period, he is given undisputed first rights to essential plumbing, even though I am standing on the rim of said plumbing, weaving and bobbing like a prize fighter to get a look at myself in the mirror over the top of Zach's head and just under Scott's armpit. As a matter of fact, when Gabe comes hopping down the hall toward the bathroom, it's as if someone yelled, "Grenade!"—with bodies flying in all directions. His aim is still not the greatest.

On the morning under discussion, Zeke was rummaging through the toothbrush can, speaking calmly in a voice that, for Zeke, was complaining.

"I spent my allowance on my own toothbrush," he frowned, "and Zach's been using it."

"I did not!" came the indignant reply.

Zeke so rarely complains that I felt it demanded an investigation and just resolution. "Rachel!" I yelled into the kitchen where Daddy's Little Princess was whittling her breakfast. "Have you been using Zeke's toothbrush?"

"Not me," was the immediate response. Why do I bother?

"Okay!" I decided to get to the bottom of the matter in the quickest way. "Bring the toothbrush can to the kitchen!" I dumped the contents on the table with a flourish that would have done Sherlock Holmes proud. "All right! Quiet! All of you. Now, pick out your own toothbrush."

I was stunned. Six little hands grabbed simultaneously for the yellow one. Zeke simply sighed. "I give up," he said and trudged to his room to finish dressing.

I risked the split second required to glance at the clock, then dove for the bedroom and my closet where, I'm sorry to confess, I neglected to coordinate my winter color palette. And since it had started to rain, I completed my stunning ensemble with Scott's knee-high mud boots. Then suddenly from the kitchen I heard a noise resembling the bellow of a large pachyderm.

I made a near perfect two point landing at the table where Gabe was spooning through a jar of peanut butter, using one of Scott's disposable razors. He was in a state of rage, staring at Rachel with glazed eyes, his neck veins distended. She, on the other hand, appeared totally unperturbed, so I directed my question to her.

"So what's the problem?" I asked. Her reply was deadpan.

"There's nuts in the peanut butter and he thinks it's *my* fault."

I confiscated the razor, gave it a quick swipe with a dish towel, and delivered it to its rightful owner in the bathroom. He accepted it with a puzzled, and somewhat pained, expression.

"Smells like peanut butter."

"Think of it as beard conditioner," I suggested.

I took a quick glance at the clock and felt the usual jolt. "Head for the station wagon!" I yelled. "We're gonna miss the bus again!" Everyone started to cry and/or scream, including Daddy, who evidently did not feel up to another careening chase over country roads trying to catch the school bus before it reached the highway and picked up speed. We had even begun to suspect that the bus driver actually *enjoyed* the chase and took pleasure in trying to outrun us.

Zeke dashed by on his way out the door, and, even in the chaos, I knew that something had to be done. I caught him in mid-stride. He was wearing cutoffs, a shirt which had obviously been rolled into a wad the night before and used to shoot baskets, no socks and a tennis shoe with a loose sole that flapped against the floor in duck-like fashion as he ran.

"Zeke," I said with remarkable calm, "I only ask one thing of you when you leave this house to go to school. By your appearance, I would like you to say to the world, 'I live in a house. I do not live under a bridge.' Go change your clothes. I'll drop you guys off at school. Daddy would never be able to catch the bus now."

Scott grinned like a kid whose dental appointment had just been canceled and darted out the door before I could change my mind. I needed to make a stop at their school sometime during the day anyway to fill out multiple immunization forms for the famous and ominous-sounding Permanent Record. The school had waited for this information as long as the state would allow, and my children were in danger of being expelled.

Why had I delayed? Well, picture this. Four children, numerous shots per child, and an absent-minded mother who doesn't even remember where her checkbook is most of the time, much less under which category she filed, "children's shots." Fortunately I remembered to look under "T" for "Traumatic Experiences." By the time I got through with the questionnaires at the school, I was so pooped I think I put "Undecided" in the blank next to Name, and "Not Applicable" in the blank by Sex.

I had brought Gabriel along with me and he had been remarkably quiet and good. Just as I started to compliment his behavior, I realized he had licked and stuck an entire book of postage stamps to the school library shelves. He was beaming at his handiwork, and I decided it had been well worth the five bucks for the stamps. After all, libraries are managed by educated people; surely they could figure out a simple way to get the stamps off the shelves without removing the finish.

I scooped Gabe up in my arms and dashed for the car, muttering aloud about all that had to be accomplished that day.

"Gabe, Momma's got to stop by the grocery store and get home in time to get Daddy some underwear washed, and I *have* to get the house cleaned today…"

As I attempted to lower him into the car seat, I felt his arms tighten around my shoulders and his warm breath on my neck.

"And love on me," he whispered in my ear.

I felt as if I'd been running at top speed and hit a wire stretched across the road. I stepped back and took a deep breath of the cool autumn air. A crimson leaf danced lazily down from an oak tree in a ballerina-like pirouette. Looking down into Gabriel's upturned face, I brushed his thick dark hair back from his forehead, marveling at how soft it was. Deep gratitude washed over me for my four-year-old, who had his priorities straight.

"Yes," I answered in a deliberately slow, purposefully soft voice as I hugged him close, "and love on you."

The early bird may get the worm, and as far as I was concerned that day, he could have it. Real people, and especially little ones, need to stop and smell the flowers along the way.

But I have stilled and quieted my soul;
like a weaned child with its mother,
like a weaned child is my soul within me.

PSALM 131:2

Worms in My Apple!

A t one point in my college education, I said to myself, "Now what I really need to do is get some practical teaching experience. All I know is what the professors tell me and what I read in books. Maybe I should do a little substitute teaching to get my feet wet." Having done so, I am extremely cautious about talking to myself anymore.

In my book, any substitute teacher who completes a full day in a new school deserves the Medal of Honor. I had been warned that this was the case. But I, you see, would be different. I had A's in all my education classes.

Furthermore, I had already survived Vacation Bible School, where I had encountered Benji, the small boy who could leap tall Sunday School shelves in a single bound. In one morning alone, this pre-schooler had held me and my shivering class of four-year-olds at bay with a spray bottle of 409 disinfectant, then proceeded to feed our rare Japanese goldfish purple Kool-Aid.™

Yes, I would not be just a conqueror, I would be more than a conqueror. I would be irresistibly creative and vivacious. Firm, yet kind. I might even sew matching outfits for the children from my old drapes and teach them to sing "Do Re Me" as I entered the room strumming my guitar. I would climb every mountain, ford every stream!

Had I known what awaited me, I probably would have joined the convent.

I enthusiastically listed my name at the administration building under available substitutes, and then waited every morning throughout the month of September for the phone to ring. Every evening in September I picked out something "teacherish" to wear, my favorite being the standard denim jumper embroidered with apples and tiny black boards and sporting little ceramic buttons in the shape of yellow school buses.

Wouldn't I be a picture? With my hair pulled back in a red gingham bow, matching ankle socks and tennis shoes painted to look like watermelons, I would have that early-childhood-educated look written all over me. Kindergarten power clothes, one might say.

I could have saved myself the trouble. My nighttime ritual of laying out clothes for the next day became an exercise in futility. Scott and the children began giving me patronizing, "Isn't she pitiful?" looks as I picked out the best read aloud stories for my hoped for students.

"What cha doin', Becky?" Scott would gently probe.

"I'm getting ready in case I get called to teach in the morning," I'd answer confidently.

Then he would give an exaggerated "Let's humor her" wink to the kids and say in a voice usually used by teachers of nursery school children, "Isn't that nice."

Then it happened. On a morning early in October the phone rang.

"Mrs. Freeman? Could you be at the Junior High in twenty minutes?"

"Oh, my!" I stuttered, not wanting to appear overly eager. "This is awfully short notice. And junior high—that's a little older than I expected—but yes, I'll be there!"

I mentally began to switch gears from kindergarten level to junior high. I had been so excited about teaching young children cute finger plays. I was soon to discover that junior high boys know some very interesting ones of their own. I reluctantly hung the jumper with the yellow school bus buttons back in the closet and opted for a purple knit dress with high heels and headed for the Junior High School. My first stop was the principal's office.

"Hi, there," I cheerfully greeted the man I assumed was the principal. He did not introduce himself.

His glance at me seemed to say, "There's one born every minute," as he came from behind the counter and headed out the door.

"Follow me," he barked. I struggled to keep up with his long strides while attempting to follow the designated lines on the floors in my dainty black pumps. I longed for my watermelon tennis shoes.

Teachers lined the hallways, apparently guarding their classroom doors. I searched their faces for a glimmer of friendliness, but found their faces screwed up as if they'd had persimmons for breakfast. And they looked old, so very, very old.

The principal stopped abruptly before an unguarded door. The sounds issuing from behind it sounded like the crowd at an exciting football game. "Smiley" opened the door and indicated I should walk through it.

"Any...anything I should know?" I dared to ask.

"There's a white button on the wall in each classroom," came the clipped reply. "Press it if you need help."

What a soothing thought for a rookie sub—panic buttons in every classroom—just like the ones used in banks to foil hold-ups. I entered the room filled with seventh graders eager to chew me up and spit me out. On my desk I found a note from the regular teacher: "Check for last night's homework. Give spelling test. Good luck." It was a place to start.

"Please," I quavered to the teeming masses, "if you don't mind, would you take out last night's homework? That is, if it's not too much trouble. Please." My voice had become that of an adolescent boy.

I waited for the class to move, to hear the rustling of papers, notebooks opening. Nothing. Just awkward silence. Could it be possible that not a single child had done their homework? Finally, mercifully, a girl in glasses and braids broke the silence.

"Anyone who doesn't bring their homework back to class needs a demerit slip filled out." This helpful child approached the teacher's desk and produced the forms and indicated I was to fill them in. They appeared to be about twenty lines long, in triplicate.

"Fine," I agreed, my smile beginning to hurt. "Now. How many of you do not have your homework this morning?" Every hand in the room shot up, with the exception of my little braided helper (who also informed me she had a perfect attendance record). So, I spent the first thirty minutes of the period filling out twenty-one demerit forms while the class played wastebasket spitball. Obviously there was not going to be time today for the creative group activities and dramatic play I had planned.

At this point, the English teacher from next door poked her wrinkled, angry face into my noisy classroom and shook a bony finger at the group.

"Don't move! Don't say another word! Don't even think of asking to go to the bathroom. I am right next door and I can see through walls! Do you hear me?!"

We were all dumb struck, including the sub, and the students nodded their heads in synchronized submission. After that, it was blessedly quiet, at least for a while. I decided it might be safe to check roll, but as I reached for the grade book, sounds of scuffling jerked me back to reality.

"Mrs. Freeman!" squealed my little braided friend. "They're fighting!" Sure enough, two boys were having at it, fists and legs flying. I knew immediately this was no job for a greenhorn and I hit the panic button. At the same time I yelled across the hall for the English teacher-cum-drill-sergeant to help me pull the combatants apart.

Thirty minutes later, long after the young warriors had been subdued, the principal appeared. He apologized for the delay and explained there had been another fight going on in another classroom and the other teacher had buzzed first. An insane vision shot through my mind of thirty teachers trying to see who can hit the panic button first, just like on the game shows.

I desperately wanted to go home. In fact, I wanted my Mommy. But alas, it was only the end of first period.

At the end of the day, when the last of the canni—I mean kids, charged out the doors, I became more resolved than ever not to teach adolescents again. Even if one or two of them *did* have a perfect attendance record. Those gifted ones would simply have to manage without me. I laid my head on the desk and tried to cry, but I was too drained. Then I became aware of a figure standing beside me.

When I looked up, I was startled. Standing before me was a grandmotherly woman with twinkling blue eyes and a wonderfully gentle voice. I thought for a moment it was an angel, but she looked vaguely familiar. Could it be? Yes, it was the English Drill Sergeant with x-ray vision who had earlier helped separate the two boys locked in what appeared to be mortal combat.

"Honey," she began, "it's not your fault. You were just too nice, that's all. I'm sorry to tell you that so many kids today only understand *tough*. Their home lives would break your heart if you knew them, but as a sub, you're going to have to learn to transfix a kid with one hard look. The drill sergeant you saw this morning—that is not me. I would much rather be nice, too, but most of the time I don't dare…" While she spoke, a horrible fear knifed through me.

"Excuse me," I managed, and rushing past the transformed woman, headed for the teacher's lounge. I stared into the mirror, my worst fears confirmed. Staring back at me was only a twisted shadow of my former self. My eyes had narrowed to slits, my face was wrinkled beyond recognition, and I looked old—so very, very old.

My breath coming in sharp gasps, I found my car and gripped the wheel tightly all the way home, relieved to see my hand on the steering wheel was smooth, not wrinkled, the nails pink and manicured rather than long, sharp, and curling. Safely home, I fell in the doorway, grabbed the phone, dialed the administration building, and instructed the startled secretary to remove my name from the substitute teacher's list for all eternity.

Pride goes before destruction,
a haughty spirit before a fall.
PROVERBS 16:18
❧

Bee Pollen and Worm Milk: The Geritol Years

Christmas Eve morning found Scott and me together shoving our youngest child into the last remaining square foot of our luggage-and-gift-packed van.

"Next year," I puffed, "let's rent a moving van, hang the expense."

Scott settled into the driver's seat. "Maybe we ought to just stay home next year," he offered, and braced for mutiny from the back of the van.

"No!" Frantic, muffled voices of children arose in unified protest. "We like to go to Grannie's house!"

Scott shrugged, started the engine, and then reached down to peel a well-licked candy cane from the seat of his brushed-denim pants. He tossed it out the window in Daisy's direction, making her day.

So, over the meadow and through the woods to Grandmother's house we went. In reality, we were *leaving* our "Little House in the Woods" to go to Grandmother's house in the 'burbs. Once we settled into Grandmother's living room on Christmas Eve, with family strewn on the floor and "Deck the Halls" playing in the background, we knew we'd be back next year.

This was to be my first Christmas with my newly married little sister, and I looked forward to cozy chats in a back bedroom where we would spend several hours alone while Mother joyfully watched over the children. Fa-la-la-la-la, it was not to be.

Mother and Daddy had just had their physicals, complete with cholesterol tests, and Mother had discovered that all those years of chocolate-covered conversations had caught up with her. There was not a chip of chocolate in the entire house!

"It rusts your pipes," Mother informed us. "Full of fat—elevates your LDL and lowers your HDL. The LDL is bad cholesterol. You can remember it as Lousy DL. HDL is the good stuff. You can remember it as Happy DL."

"I must not be old enough to be interested," I muttered, but she was already on the way to the kitchen to get her and Daddy's cholesterol-lowering niacin tablets. She brought his to him, along with a glass of water, as he lounged in his easy chair with a look on his face that was borderline rebellious.

"They make me turn red and tingle," he protested. "I think they may be dangerous."

"That's ridiculous," she insisted. "The whole world is taking niacin to lower their cholesterol. What makes you think you'd be the first fatality?" She shoved the water and the pills at him. "Drink up!" To us she commented, "This is a man who has never had a minor illness—all major." She turned to retrieve what she expected to be an empty glass, but found Daddy still examining the large blue and white capsule in the palm of his hand, the glass still full to the brim.

"I don't think I'm gonna take 'em anymore," he said, looking as if he were prepared to deal with the consequences, which were not long in coming.

"All right!" she declared, retrieving the pill and the glass before flouncing to the kitchen. "I'm tired of arguing with you. I do not intend to chase you around the house trying to get you to take your vitamins anymore! You're on your own from this day forward!"

"I'll take my chances," he called after her. He turned to us and grinned. "I think I saw her using my tackle box to sort and store our pills in this morning."

Their fuss was about as serious as most I'd ever seen between them and lasted about as long. We spent Christmas Eve sprawled in the living room floor, playing games, working puzzles, and humming harmony to carols issuing from the stereo. Mother was in rare form with a fresh audience of grandchildren, performing her repertoire of all nine verses of, "Up on the House-top," each verse sung in a different, and more exaggerated, foreign accent.

We had a late, light supper which Mother served on their 1950s metal TV trays. When we had eaten every morsel and crumb available to us, Daddy took his coffee cup and ran it back and forth across his metal tray in the manner of prison inmates raking tin cups across cell bars to incite rebellion.

"Is this all the swill we get?" he demanded.

"Oh, for Pete's sake," Mother shot back, "you ate it too fast. If you chew food slower, you eat a lot less. You sounded like a dinosaur in a feeding frenzy. I think I'll start calling you, 'Tyrannasaurus.'"

He flirtatiously winked his eye. "*You* can call me Rex," he invited.

While they held onto each other and laughed so hard their eyes watered, my sister and I seized the opportunity to steal away and scrounge the kitchen for *anything* that might contain sugar. We found an old crunchy fudge diet bar in the dark recesses of the cabinet and hungrily divided it between us. After one bite, Rachel handed me her half in disgust.

"That stuff tastes like chocolate-covered cat food!"

"Meow," I purred, and stuffed her reject in my mouth before she could change her mind.

Mother and Daddy went off to bed, reminding Scott and me that, in case we had forgotten batteries for any of the toys Santa was to bring, the city version of Get-It-Kwik closed at midnight.

At about 1:00 A.M., Mr. and Mrs. Santa fell into a deep sleep, dreaming of a three-layered chocolate cake with french vanilla ice cream topped with hot fudge. Dawn arrived all too soon.

Gabe was already shooting up the place with the latest superhero toy. Our only daughter had dressed and re-dressed her doll, while Zach and Zeke gazed in wonder at pellet guns. Amid the clamor, the doorbell rang and I headed in that direction.

The doorbell ringer turned out to be the neighbor from across the street, who had noticed our van's sliding door ajar and, seeing its jumbled interior, assumed it had been ransacked during the night. Scott followed him out to the street to check it out and then had to explain to the neighbor, a bachelor, that the van was exactly as we had left it the night before.

In spite of all this activity, Mother and Daddy were not up yet. The kitchen remained dark and quiet, which was most unusual.

Thirty minutes later, when Rachel and Gilley staggered into the kitchen to figure out how to operate Mother's coffee pot, Daddy emerged from the bedroom with an odd expression on his face. I couldn't figure out if he was distressed or amused.

"Your mother isn't feeling well," he said, stifling a twitch at the corners of his mouth. "She's had a rough night. She's been regurgitating excess niacin since about 2:00 this morning."

Rachel and I managed to get Christmas brunch together and Mother emerged from her niacin overdose somewhat chastened but nevertheless determined to bound into her twilight years with vim, vigor and vitality, taking Daddy with her—pushing, pulling, and dragging if necessary.

After the holidays, I went out to eat with Mother and Daddy. Mother had loved dining out in cafeterias for years, originally because they made great pies. Now, however, it was because they offered a glittering array of salads and cooked veggies brimming with vitamins and beta carotene. I observed that cafeterias seem to be primarily populated by people their age or older, and that most couples swap bites, trade food, drink each other's tea and coffee, and share plates as if they were playing a rhythmic game of musical food. At one point, Daddy directed Mother to, "Put the chicken on the bread plate," and she responded with a toe tapping, "Pickin' out dough, honor your partner and do-si-do!" They both laughed until they had to wipe their eyes with their napkins.

"The first sign of aging," I observed, "is a gradual loss of dignity and decorum." Unperturbed, they sat there grinning at each other with an air of, "Ain't Life Grand?"

They looked so happy and rested. I felt a new anticipation for the years when Scott and I would be dancing *our* jig once our family responsibilities were behind us.

"Well," I threatened, "if you two keep acting this way, they may not let you room together at the nursing home."

Indeed, if they should ever be separated, Mother will probably waste away to skin and bones. She seems to feel that food eaten from Daddy's plate will not make her fat, and coffee from his cup will not keep her awake. I have come to understand the primary reason for all this sharing of food is to cut calories and cost, and I have certainly noticed they seem a bit more cost conscious these days. They have discovered, seemingly with shock, that they are within a few short years of retirement.

Mother has begun assembling an impressive assortment of vitamin bottles to keep expensive doctors away. She suffers agony every time she must remove the cotton from a new vitamin bottle and throw it away. Such a waste! One evening, in a flash of inspiration, she decided to use the cotton to apply her skin toner.

Daddy had already gone to bed and turned out the lights when she lay down beside him. Soon his doleful voice broke the stillness.

"I knew it was going to happen."

"What was going to happen?" she demanded.

"You smell like a giant vitamin pill!"

And the man said,
the woman whom thou gavest to be with me,
she gave me of the tree, and I did eat.
GENESIS 3:12, KJV

Welcome to My Classworm!

On an unusually cool and pleasant August Saturday after-noon in 1991, I walked across a stage to accept a college diploma in elementary education. Following the ceremony, amidst joyful celebration with our family, I presented to my husband and our four children their own versions of a diploma, handmade for them by their Aunt Laura. I assured them it was not just *my* degree that had been earned, but *our* degree, and I framed and hung their "diplomas" beside my own.

It was an emotional and enormously significant day for me, and the words of a poem danced through my mind often that day and in the days that followed. It read:

The only crown I ask, Dear Lord,
To wear is this: That I may teach a little child.

I do not ask that I may ever stand
Among the wise, the worthy or the great;
I only ask that softly, hand in hand,
A child and I may enter at the gate.

ANONYMOUS

After a wonderful student teaching experience, I had regained the confidence I had lost from the experience with substitute teaching. There is nothing like hands-on experience and I felt proud to belong to a profession that encourages mentoring. You might say I was pretty idealistic, having never actually been shut up in a room alone with small children for an entire school year. A major concern at the time was whether I could keep up with my own lunch money, much less the education of twenty-plus students.

So far I had not been able to interest my own child, Gabe, in learning his *ABC's*, but I kept trying to sneak up on his blind side. After all, kindergarten with its confinement was definitely in his near future. Would he be able to accept the bit and bridle?

"Gabe," I approached one afternoon, "next year you will go to kindergarten and you will get to learn to read!"

"Yeah," he responded with gusto, "and *this* year I get to play on the dock and have fun!" Oh well, in our years at home together I *had* taught him to snap his fingers, to whistle, and to blow a great bubble.

And by the grace of God, we had some years at home together before I entered the work force. As a teacher, I would still be able to be home when the children were home. It seemed the best solution to our economic stress and we looked forward to being a two paycheck family. And to be truthful, I was eager to get a real classful of those little heartwormers and hear them say in harmonic chorus, "Good morning, Mrs. Freeman!" Wasn't *nobody* gonna burst my bubble!

With my guitar tucked under one arm, my "Teacher's Have Class" tote bag snuggled under the other, I took a deep breath and swung open the door labeled, "Mrs. Freeman's First Grade Adventurers," and turned on the light as if I had just directed the sun to rise.

The room was perfect. It was clean and bright, with discovery centers inviting pint-sized exploration. My favorite spot was the large, homey corner by the flower trimmed window. There I had placed a huge rug, a rocking chair, and a book shelf. I set the guitar down gently in the reading nook, wrote my name on the chalkboard in three-inch script, and turned to face my first day of teaching.

I was soon to discover there were a few things they neglected to cover in Education 404. First of all, twenty-five students arrived simultaneously when I had been expecting seventeen. Each of the twenty-five students was escorted by an average of five family members. I had not realized how exciting the first day of school is in rural areas hard up for entertainment.

I managed somehow to finally reassure the last momma, daddy, sissy, Aunt Elsie Pearl, and Cousin Billy Bob that Little Bubba would be in the hands of an expert. They could go home. Please.

Turning to face my new students, I planned to jump right into our getting to know you activities, but someone was knocking at my classroom door.

It was the lead first grade teacher giving me advance warning about the horrors of the first day of bus run. She strongly advised I take care of that order of business first off. As Ross Perot is fond of saying, "Here's the deal": 3,498 look-alike buses descend upon our school in the afternoon, and each of my rookie first graders would have to find his/her particular bus—with the help of his/her rookie teacher. My job was to assign each child to the correct bus, colored name tag, sidewalk picture, and bus run teacher. I approached one of my little students for a sample information-gathering interview.

"Sweetheart, do you know your bus number?"

"Yes," the little fellow replied with all the confidence in the world. "It is black and it is stuck on the side of a yellow bus. I like it." He seemed satisfied he had given me all the information I needed.

"Okay..." I persisted, "do you know where you live, Darlin'?"

"Yes'm. I live 'cross the street from my friend."

I kept on ringin', but this child was not pickin' up the phone. "What about your telephone number? Can you tell me that?"

"Uh-huh. 1-2-3-4-5-7-8-9. I brought a show and tell in my backpack." Surely enough, he had.

"Oh, my...a real live frog. Named Ralph, you say? That's great." Wondering how on earth I was going to get this child home at the end of the day, I asked hopefully, "Is Ralph, by any chance, a *homing* amphibian?"

Seeing the other natives were getting restless, I decided to deal with bus run later. I reached for my guitar, and re-captured their attention by strumming a chord or two. I smiled broadly and broke into song.

"Oh, what a beautiful morning," I trilled. Just before I got to my favorite line—"Everything's going my way"—there was another tapping at my chamber door. It was the principal, Mrs. Boone, reminding me to do lunch count. How could I have forgotten?

While the children entertained themselves by sampling bites of fresh Play Doh™ and playing jab thy neighbor with freshly sharpened pencils, I glanced at what appeared to be the IRS version of the long lunch form. I never dreamed there could be so many lunching possibilities. There was your free lunch, your reduced lunch, your charged lunch, your paid lunch, your brought lunch, your brought lunch milk buyers, your brought lunch with milk and ice cream, your paid lunch with ice cream, and finally, your individual milk and ice cream buyers. Each possibility came with its own cute little code.

I did my best, but my head began to throb. Mrs. Boone sent down her executive secretary with a calculator, and managed to get lunch count turned in sometime around 2:00 P.M., well after the big event.

During my much anticipated afternoon break, I learned I had a phone call waiting for me in the office. It was Scott, informing me that Gabriel had not been allowed to start school that morning because he did not have his birth certificate.

"Okay," I said with remarkable calm, "I don't know where I put it. Tell his teacher I will be by this afternoon to show her my stretch marks in lieu of the certificate."

The highlight of the day was reading, "The Gingerbread Man," to my class and going on an explore-the-school walk as we tried to find the escaped cookie boy (whom I had cleverly dropped off earlier in the school cafeteria). One of the things I like most about six-year-olds is their complete gullibility. They were very sincere as they investigated the place, asking everyone they saw in the hall if they had seen a flat, runaway boy made of sugar and spice. When we found our giant cookie friend, none of the girls could bear to eat the poor thing while the boys fought over who would get to eat his eyes and head and bite off his feet.

At the end of the longest day I had ever lived, our vice-principal, Mr. Manley, peeked in to remind me to bring my bus run clipboard along when it was time for the children to board the bus. I suppose by then, word had gotten around that I needed plenty of reminders from my superiors if disaster was to be averted.

Observing Mr. Manley, I certainly thought he was a guy who lived up to his name. He was huge, with a moustache and a bald head, and I was intimidated just standing in his presence. (I later learned he is simply an overgrown teddy bear.)

But, in the five minutes that lapsed between his stern reminder and my time to venture forth leading students to the buses, I had forgotten what it was he had said I was to bring with me. In a last minute panic, I grabbed my purse and took my place with the children outside. My purse dangled from my arm where the clipboard should have been. Mr. Manley passed by and noted the purse.

"Mrs. Freeman," he observed dryly, "you're not planning to ride the bus home *with* the children, are you?"

Two months into the term, I was still absentmindedly carrying my purse out to bus run duty on the average of once a week. In the interim, Mr. Manley had taken to calling me, "Blondie," because he was sure that underneath my brunette exterior, there was a true dumb blonde. However, I reminded Mr. Manley that there had been moments when my purse had come in handy. Once I had saved the day when he was desperate for a pencil and I dug an eyeliner pencil from the depths of my purse.

He reminded me I had also worn one red shoe and one black shoe to school earlier in the year, totally oblivious of it until my students pointed it out to me around 9:00 A.M. Black and brown he might have excused as a plausible mistake, but black and red?

He also reminded me he had lost count of the times he had called me on the intercom to pick up my now famous purse at the office. He calculated I had accidentally left it in every major room in the building at one time or another.

He then reminded me that on both of his "walk-through" evaluations of my class, the children were straightening up the room (and dancing) to the tune of "Achy Breaky Heart."

Then I reminded Mr. Manley that I had made small children and large vice-principals laugh, which must surely be worth something. The gentle giant smiled his moustached Manley smile and gave me one of his famous bear hugs.

"You're okay, kid," he said, and moved his massive frame on down the hall.

After those lavish words of praise, my feet barely hit the ground. After I was chosen teacher of the month by my peers, I knew true job satisfaction. This is what it's all about, I decided.

That afternoon after school, I lay across my bed in what had become my usual state of exhaustion, and I felt Gabe snuggle next to me. I dreamily observed he looked awfully cute in the new school clothes I had bought him with my first paycheck.

"Momma?" he asked, "would it be okay if I just lay here by you and pretend you can hear me?"

Oh, God! I cried out silently as I encircled my lonely little boy with all the strength I had left, *What am I doing?!*

Even in laughter the heart may ache,
and joy may end in grief.
PROVERBS 14:13

Glowworms

L ast Thanksgiving, our family decided to meet at a lake in Kentucky, one day's drive for each of us. David and his wife, Barb, brought their three-year-old Tyler from Indiana, but Rachel and Gilley declined to be incarcerated in their small car for a day with tiny Trevor. Tyler met Grannie and Daddy George at the door, his enormous brown eyes wide with excitement as he spied the mammoth bucket of flavored popcorn his grand-parents were hauling up the steps.

Imagine Tyler's disappointment when he discovered only a few kernels left in the container. There is no such thing as sinless perfection and sometimes, Mother and Daddy descend into gluttony. Seeing our reproachful eyes, Mother tried to explain.

"How can I tell you that you cannot trust two sensible, people with ten gallons of popcorn on a long trip in a small car?"

We allowed her time to put away her coat and get a cup of coffee before we began interrogating. Her defense was inspired.

"We hadn't been on the road two hours before I began struggling with visions of caramel flavored popcorn. I reached into the back where the can occupied half the seat and grabbed a handful to share with Daddy George.

"Before long, we were filling the lid of the can one load at a time, our hands moving from lid to mouth with increasing speed. Soon the rate of speed was such that our hands could not be seen—similar to the blades of a helicopter in flight; two rotors are in motion, but only a blur is visible." (By this time our four children and Tyler were open mouthed, and Mother warmed to her story.)

"Finally, with so many trips to the back seat for refills, the car started to wobble on the highway. My accomplice suggested I try to get the entire can into the front seat with us, but I was not willing to hang out the door in order to accommodate the can. When he suggested I do so, I knew we had to get control of ourselves." She paused dramatically and gazed at the kids.

"I reminded Daddy George of you *dear* children. Our rotor blades slowed and again became hands as they finally sputtered to a belching halt. But then, we made a terrible mistake." She paused for effect.

"We were thirsty and stopped for a tall glass of water. The popcorn, acting like a million tiny sponges, swelled up until only one of us could ride in the car. Daddy George had to tie me on top of the car for the rest of the trip!"

The kids loved it, but Zach and Zeke, so close to being worldly-wise, groaned a lot. "Awww, Grannie..." We may not have been able to transport a turkey to Kentucky for our Thanksgiving table, but there was plenty of ham to go around, thanks to Grannie.

We had a great time, with a snowfall sufficient to build a slightly muddy snowman, but insufficient to deter the fishermen. They sat hunkered down on the dock in the falling snow, pulling in dumb fish who didn't know it was too cold to bite. We fried their catch on Friday night, as Uncle David did his stellar imitation of a Cajun chef.

"Fuhst, you take 'bout half a pound a buttuh dat what cum from da she-cow…" Barb became Mother's "extra pair of hands" as Mother liked to describe her, while I loved up on Tyler.

"I've decided," Mother announced, "that if we checked Barb over thoroughly we'd find a label somewhere that reads, 'Made in heaven especially for David.'"

Saturday morning we packed and loaded the cars and then gathered in the living room for a precious tradition. The kids lounged on the rug, we grown-ups sat in an easy circle, our eyes meeting and holding one another's, storing up pictures of dear faces we would not see again for several months. Quiet settled over us, and Daddy reached for Mother's hand on his right, my hand on his left and the circle became connected.

"Lord Jesus," he began, "we're grateful for You and Your presence here with us. We know you've enjoyed it as much as we have. We ask that You go before and behind us on the road; surround each of us with Your protection. Bless our children with continued love and laughter. Draw them close to Your heart. Prosper their way. And may our grandchildren grow as You grew—'in wisdom and in stature and in favor with God and men.' We love You, Lord. Amen."

And Israel beheld Joseph's sons, and said, Who are these?
And Joseph said unto his father,
They are my sons, whom God hath given me in this place.
And he said,
Bring them, I pray thee, unto me, and I will bless them.

GENESIS 48:8-9, KJV
∾

Weary Worms

By mid-term, I had come to see life more clearly than ever before. I now knew what I truly wanted. After a full day of dealing with first graders, I had only two desires: (1) sleep, and (2) being left alone.

I was rarely privileged to be alone, even at the grocery store, which may have been for the best because I could never remember where I parked the car. If the children could not remember, then our poor sack boy was doomed to roam the parking lot with us, pushing a cart sufficiently full of groceries to feed a family of six robust eaters for two weeks. On one occasion, our sack boy paused momentarily to wipe the sweat from his brow, and in the awkward pause, I felt I should say something.

"I bet this happens to you all the time—people not remembering where they parked their cars?"

"No, ma'am," he replied politely.

I did develop a system of grocery shopping such that I could remain in a state near to dozing. I pass it on to other exhausted moms; use it with my blessing.

The method requires no menu planning at all. I call it "Zombie Shopping." I amble into the supermarket, lean against a post until a sharp-looking mother with apparently healthy children pushes her cart down the aisle, and I then fall in behind her. Whatever she puts into her basket, I put into mine. After all, her children look well-fed.

I had grocery shopping down but my marriage was leaking at every fitting and threatening to blow sky high under the pressure. My vision of Scott and me jogging happily together in our middle years began to seem remote indeed. We weren't even laughing between fights anymore, they were coming in such rapid succession. We were both heartsick, scared to death it would never be wonderful again.

It was a dismal winter, reminding me of another difficult winter two years before when my Nonnie died. She had lived to be eighty-six years old. The last eight of those years had brought senility and illness, and eventually she had to live in a nursing home. She had changed so much physically and mentally that it would have been impossible for someone who had known her in the past to recognize her. Even so, it was hard to let her go.

Mother's big family re-assembled itself in the small West Texas town where they had all grown up. We gathered in the church where Nonnie had been a faithful member for fifty-two years. Because Nonnie's home place had been sold, and there was no house where we could all be together, we stayed in motels the night before the funeral. On the day of the funeral, those people in the church who had known the family for half a century served us a wonderful meal in the church fellowship hall, and opened their large, lovely parlor for us to use for the afternoon.

In the few minutes before we were to enter the sanctuary for the service, Mother put her arm around my shoulders and looked down the aisle we would soon walk to where Nonnie lay in state at the front of the flower-laden room.

"Becky," Mother whispered, her eyes brimming and her voice husky. "She is lying in almost the exact spot where Daddy and I were married thirty-six years ago. What memories this place holds!" As I thought of what was happening with Scott and me, the contrast with my parents' happy marriage was almost too painful to think about.

Then the music began and the usher signaled the family to move into the sanctuary and take our seats. After a small, hidden choir of Nonnie's friends sang two of her favorite hymns—"No Tears in Heaven," and "Where the Soul Never Dies,"—Daddy stepped to the podium to read the eulogy Mother had written two days before.

> In an era when the concept of a woman totally dedicated to motherhood is rapidly fading from memory, it would be supremely wasteful to allow the passing of Elsie Jones to occur without thoughtfully savoring what it has meant to be her child, or her grandchild, or her great-grandchild.
>
> In an era when the world is starving for a friend who can simply be there for us when we need them, who knows what it means to listen with complete self-forgetfulness, and who somehow brings comfort by their very presence, it would be a great loss not to pause and reflect on the life of Elsie Jones and her example of being this kind of friend.
>
> Her six living children will have different memories because they were born over a fourteen-year span of time. The older ones will remember the comfort and stability she brought to them as adolescents during the desperately hard and bitter years of the Depression—how she could make a pot of red beans and a pan of corn bread taste as good as a steak dinner—how she could make the light from a kerosene lamp seem brighter, and the cold winds blowing across the

New Mexico prairie not quite so biting. To be sure, there was heartache enough to share at times, but there was always a mother's quiet and constant love.

And as the five boys grew older, the horseplay and hilarity almost raised the roof. They teased her until she blushed and laughingly scolded. They never missed an opportunity to untie her apron strings in passing. It was not unusual for one of them, fully grown, to sit in her lap while the rest of us enjoyed the show—including Nonnie.

When the grandchildren began to come along, she somehow managed to make all thirteen of them feel as if they were special. And of course, to her, they were. We were privileged to have Nonnie for so many years and privileged that her grandchildren were able to come home to her even as young adults and find healing for their wounds. Again, not so much by her words of wisdom, but by her quiet listening and her indescribable ability to comfort just by being there.

To her children's spouses, she became more mother than mother-in-law, especially when, with the passing of time, they lost their own mothers.

Here Daddy's voice broke, and it took a minute for him to continue.

And when she was old and infirm, she considered them her sons and daughters. But more than that, they were her friends.

So many were her friends, and many of you gathered here today became family for her, especially when she was growing old and her children could not be with her all the time. Often you made your way to the doorstep of the white house trimmed in blue paint and decorated with red geraniums to enjoy a good hot cup of coffee with her. And you found that same indefinable comfort, solace, and strength to go on.

In later years, you made your way to her house to deliver groceries, or to take her where she needed to go, or to make repairs, or do chores around the house. In your turn, you gave *her* comfort and solace and strength to go on.

And go on she did. It is one of the paradoxes of life that old age comes to us at a time when we just don't feel like handling it, but when she had to give up the house she had enjoyed so very much and leave her home town of more than fifty years, she did it with grace and strength, making the difficult adjustment to life in her children's homes.

She has left so many of us with a precious heritage: that there can be love and laughter in the bitterest of times; that there is tremendous power in a meek and quiet spirit; that there is healing both in listening silence and in a gentle word and touch; that *all* things in life can be used to mold us into the gentle benediction her life became.

Thank you so much for being here today to honor her with us.

From somewhere above us, the choir began to sing the old hymn, "Whispering Hope," another favorite of my Nonnie's.

Soft as the voice of an angel,

Breathing a lesson unheard,

Hope with a gentle persuasion

Whispers her comforting word:

Wait till the darkness is over,

Wait till the tempest is done,

Hope for the sunshine tomorrow,

After the shower is gone.

Going back in memory to that Saturday afternoon in a little church in a dusty West Texas town, I saw a bit more clearly what I *really* wanted to be when I grew up, and I realized the monumental task before me to achieve it. Maybe there was still hope for sunshine tomorrow, though it seemed at the moment the shower would never go away. But, my Nonnie always said it would be so.

I have been reminded of your sincere faith,
which first lived in your grandmother Lois
and in your mother Eunice and,
I am persuaded, now lives in you also.

2 TIMOTHY 1:5
୭

Wormin' My Way
Back to You

The counselor leaned back and lounged in his chair as is the manner of good counselors. Scott and I began our tales of woe, and before long he snapped bolt upright in his chair. Undeterred, we continued unburdening ourselves. He eventually shook his head in wonder and probably broke the cardinal rule of marriage counseling by looking shocked.

"You two really *don't* know how to communicate very well, do you?" he observed.

I, personally, was insulted. I knew *I* could talk a blue streak and Scott had a college degree in communications. Once the guy got his equilibrium back, he helped us see we had a lot of pride to swallow, and we slowly began to nourish our relationship back to health. In the process, we tried several techniques our counselor suggested—some helpful, some hilarious, and some downright humiliating.

I loved the write out your feelings technique. As a writer, I could pen my spouse to the wall any day. Scott began to receive reams of overnight mail from me; I left it waiting in his truck to be reviewed in the morning after an evening's argument. I must say, I had the art of sounding maritally correct down to a science, especially on paper. My defense would resemble a well-prepared legal brief with plenty of melodrama thrown in for good measure. One morning in return for one of my lengthy and brilliant treatises, I found the following note stuck to the coffee pot: "Dear Becky, I hate your shirt. Love, Scott."

With the mirror technique, one partner is to listen actively to the spouse and then repeat back word for word what the spouse just said. On the other hand, role-playing involves pretending one is, for example, the mother of the other while he or she vents old frustrations at the role-player. We found both of these absolutely impossible to carry out with a straight face, but I heartily recommend them for the comic relief they provide.

The help your man meet your needs technique works well for us, and actually, I made this one up all by myself. When I find myself in need of a hug or words of affection, I locate Scott and put my arms around his neck.

Then I say, "You think I'm so sweet and pretty you can hardly keep your eyes off me, don't you?" He can't resist a smile and obediently nods. I am fulfilled and happy. Actually, he reports that my putting words in his mouth causes him to realize he really does *feel* the words. So—I am working on this line next: "Scott, you just love cute, nicely-rounded women. You'd hate to see me lose an ounce, wouldn't you, sweetheart?"

Other exercises and experiences have helped too, but they must wait for my authoritative self-help book, *We're Happily Married and We Haven't Figured out Exactly Why*. Probably it has a lot to do with just getting our minds back on each other again.

All we can say is, we thank the good Lord every day for helping two starry-eyed kids keep their promise to each other.

I can't imagine we would ever take the wonder of a good marriage for granted again. To put it in simple country terms, we had the socks scared off us. I had been awakened out of my sleep-walking state, and I knew I wanted more than anything else in the world for my family to be intact—and not just intact, but as happy as possible. How could I give it my best shot when I was almost always exhausted? On the other hand, how were we going to be a happy family when there was a large financial shortfall every month?

I will never forget the moment I made the "Big Decision."

I had gone to a ladies' retreat with a group from our church and was sitting in the audience listening to a good friend describe her marriage to an alcoholic husband. For years, she put off having children, taking the financial burden of supporting herself and her husband on her own shoulders. Eventually they had a baby and she continued to juggle a full-time career and a family. She stood at the podium, tears standing in her eyes, as she spoke softly.

"I thought there was no way out, that I had no choice but to keep working. But then one day I felt the Lord speaking to me in my heart.

"'What would happen if you just quit? What would happen if you just stepped out in faith and trusted Me to provide?'"

As she spoke, I felt my heart jump. The words, "What if…" echoed in my own mind. Then she finished her story.

"There were some difficult adjustments, and I won't kid you, it has been a financial strain. But when I handed my husband the role of sole provider for the first time in our marriage, his whole attitude changed. Today he is sober and growing in the Lord. He has incredible patience with me. He has become the leader in our home and every day I think, *God, it's a miracle!*

A miracle. What a novel idea. Maybe I could get one of those.

I drove home from the retreat faster than I should have, waded through piles of papers waiting to be graded, stacks of laundry waiting to be folded, and found Scott in the kitchen. He was making sad sandwiches for the kids using bologna with rigor mortis and lettuce with no pulse, slapping the stuff onto bread the texture of croutons.

I took him by both hands, led him to the hammock outside, pulled both of us into it, and announced triumphantly, "I'm quitting work!" He exhaled at length and started to speak, but I was hot on the campaign trail now.

"Look, Scott, our family life can't get any worse than it is right now. We're microwaving underwear to get it dry in time to wear it and eating stuff out of the refrigerator that looks like it needs a shave.

"I'm sending up the white flag, throwing in the towel. This camel's back is broken, this filly won't ride, this heifer won't milk, (deep breath) not gonna do it anymore. How else can I say it?

"I have only so much time and energy to give and when I'm working, I have nothing left for the people I love the most. No one is mindin' the store around here! Whatever the cost, we *have* to find a way to get me home again."

Scott blinked twice and asked, "Is that it?"

"Yep," I answered, bracing for another round.

"Okay," he said.

"*What?*" I said.

"Okay," he repeated slowly. "We need you. To be honest, I'm relieved. And that's a surprise to me, too. We'll find a way to make it."

The stars came out in the sky above the lake and I relaxed against him. In just three more months I could be at home again with my family. It seemed far too good to be true. I checked to see if I might not be glowing in the moonlight. We swung contentedly in the hammock and smooched until Rachel hollered to us from the back door.

"Gabe just lost his baby tooth in his sandwich!"

So do not worry, saying, "What shall we eat?"
or "What shall we drink?" or "What shall we wear?"
For the pagans run after all these things,
and your heavenly Father knows that you need them.
But seek first his kingdom and his righteousness,
and all these things will be given to you as well.
Therefore do not worry about tomorrow,
for tomorrow will worry about itself.
Each day has enough trouble of its own.

MATTHEW 6:31-34

·

Homeworm Bound

After turning in my letter of resignation stating I would not renew my contract for the following year, I experienced a short period of doubt. Was I a quitter? Did I simply have a short attention span? Was I wasting my college degree? What about the sacrifices my family had made to help me get through college? Would I be able to face being a retired teacher after nine long months of faithful service? What about the students I had come to love? Didn't those children need me?

Proverbs 14:1 provided my reassurance. "The wise woman builds her house, but with her own hands the foolish one tears hers down." Yes, I was making a wise decision. My house was in desperate need of repair and a woman's touch. I would finish out the school year, then I would close that chapter of my life and open up to what the Lord would have me do at home.

Once it was settled, I felt a tremendous sense of relief and much of the pressure was off. The remaining weeks of teaching were some of the most fulfilling as I observed the progress my students had made in their learning. During the week of standardized testing, I explained to the children that they would be answering many questions for the test people.

"I want you to do your very best and color the dot by the sentence you think best answers their questions," I instructed. After the third grueling day of testing, one little boy named Christopher (beautiful blue eyes, lashes a mile long) looked up in disgust.

"The test people sure must be lazy to make a bunch of little kids work this hard to tell them answers to stuff they could find out their selves if they would just go to school."

After the days of testing were over, I thought it would be downhill all the way to the last day of school and retirement. The only remaining hurdle was the innocuously named event called field day.

My students had gone on to the playing field under the supervision of Mrs. Nuefeld, the only parent to show up that day. There they waited with excitement for Mrs. Freeman, femininity personified, to get the athletic contests going.

The first challenge I faced was to transport two ice chests at once across the school parking lot to load into my van with the ultimate goal of unloading the chests at the playing field. One of the ice chests brimmed with iced down soda pops and the second was loaded with water balloons to be used in one of the main events.

Naively, I had assumed I would have plenty of parent helpers, since I had sent heroic Mrs. Nuefeld on ahead with my class to the playing field. Evidently the parents were better acquainted with field day than I. Not a single parent was in sight, and I began to suspect the main event might be about to take place on the school parking lot with Mrs. Freeman being the sole contestant.

I managed to push, heave, and shove until, miraculously, I had one heavy ice chest atop the other on the dolly. But when I began rolling the dolly across the pavement toward my van, it started to weave in spite of my best efforts. Spectators began assembling at the school's office window. I understand from later accounts that a collective gasp ascended when I finally tripped and both ice chest lids flew open, sending fifty cans of pop clattering about over the parking lot and underneath faculty cars. A myriad of brightly colored water balloons bounced and popped among the cans, like kernels of popcorn, making blurping noises as they prematurely spewed forth their contents.

I sat down on the pavement, shoulders shaking like a leaf. The faculty watching from the window decided they were observing a nervous breakdown in progress and immediately dispatched Carl, the school counselor, to my aid. Once Carl determined I was laughing rather than crying, my audience was shocked to see him sit down on the pavement and join in my hysteria. I will have to say, he *is* an effective counselor. With his help, I was able to get on my feet, reload the sodas and the few remaining water balloons back into the ice chests and then, a few minutes later, unload them at the playing field.

I had also to unload a ten-gallon drinking can filled with orange Kool-aid™, and as I waddled from the van to the picnic table, I unwittingly pressed the spigot against my abdomen. By the time I made it to the track, I was not a pretty sight. I had begun the morning wearing a white pantsuit. I arrived at the track wearing brilliant orange Kool-aid.™ To protect myself against a monster Texas sunburn, I donned a sunbonnet in a fetching, neon shade of pink. Even from across the field, the children recognized me immediately.

"It's Mrs. Freeman!" they all cried at once. They ran to meet me and hugged me around the waist and came away with sticky orange faces and arms. "Can we have snow cones now? Huh, please, can we?"

Feeling badly about having left them waiting for so long, I consented, not thinking about setting a limit on the number of syrupy cones they could each consume. Before I realized it, the blankets we were to sit on during breaks were covered with kids and cones. I had a virtual sugar orgy on my hands.

I looked around furtively, wondering how to get control of the situation and immediately noticed the disapproving frowns aimed in my direction from the other teachers. They, of course, had wisely told their children to wait until after lunch for dessert. Forget lunch. I would have been smart if I had held out until after the athletic events.

After endless crabwalks, tricycle races, and sack hops, lunch time arrived. All the other classes organized their picnic areas, with room mothers handing out food, napkins, and drinks in a synchronized rhythm. On our blanket, however, food was the last thing on my students' minds. It was the lunch *sacks* we were interested in, for we had our own unique contest going.

"Shaun has thrown up *seven* times, Mrs. Freeman!" announced Jacoby. "That's the most of anybody!" She held tightly to Shaun's hand as if he were a prize trophy. Amazingly, Shaun was grinning. Though green around the gills, he was obviously proud of his accomplishment.

About this time, Mr. Manley strolled by. He was to be promoted and transferred to another school in the coming year. Running into me on the field in all my kaleidoscope of color caused him to glow with appreciation, as if he had had a stroke of great good fortune.

"Freeman," he said to me with a tinge of sadness I could only assume was sincere, "I'm gonna miss you next year. It's going to be like a dadgum divorce." Then he wiped an imaginary tear from one eye, turned dramatically, and whistled back toward the school building. If he hadn't been such a big man, I would have sworn I saw him skip once or twice.

Mercifully, the last day of school arrived. I scanned the children, trying to store up memories. They would forever be special to me: they were not only my first class, they were possibly my last, at least for a very long time.

My gaze settled on Dustin, my tiny, hyperactive challenge, who amazed me daily with deep and insightful questions by the zillion and just generally drove me crazy. I turned to observe my no-nonsense Chris and was reminded of the day when I had persuaded Scott to dress up as Johnny Appleseed and visit my class, complete with a tin pan cap. I had asked Chris to suggest a place where we "might put Johnny Appleseed" in our crowded room, and he responded dryly, "Why don't you lay him out on the reading table over there? He's been dead two hundred years."

And Jacoby. Would there ever be another Jacoby? Jacoby is a she, the shortest girl in the class, of stocky build, who feared no one. She had fallen in love with sweet, shy, and tall Howard, who was temporarily looking rather goofy while waiting for a front tooth to fall out.

One day, Jacoby and Howard had found two worms on the playground and had adopted them. The two clever children named them—surprise, surprise—Howard and Jacoby. The two worms occupied our science table for weeks, and no two worms were ever loved more dearly, except possibly Gabe's.

I glanced on toward Brian, whose ready smile could light up his entire face, but who often cried just as easily. I had not understood why, until Christmas time when I asked the children to write their wish lists to Santa. Brian wrote for a very long time, then, while my back was turned, stapled his letter closed with about thirty staples.

I was not happy with Brian, because I needed to read over his work before it was sealed, and I told him so. While Brian went on to P.E. class, I pulled out all the staples, grumbling all the while. When I read what he had written, I felt as if I'd taken a blow to the pit of my stomach.

"Deer Santuh," it read, "All I want is my dad to cum bak home. But mom won't let him. If you cood maik mom luv him thats ol I want for Chrismis."

I sat for a minute getting myself together, then sprinted to the gym, stood in the wide doorway, and motioned for Brian to come with me. We marched hand in hand to the teacher's lounge where I let him put quarters in the vending machines until we had candy and pop enough for the both of us. Then I pulled him onto my lap.

"Honey, I'm sorry I fussed at you about the staples. And I'm awful sorry about your daddy being gone." He relaxed against me and I tightened my arms about him. "You know, Santa can't do just everything. But no matter what happens at Christmas, Brian, remember I love you and so does Jesus. And we always will." He buried his head in my neck and cried a bit. We both did. Then we dried our tears and ate candy and drank Coke™, and by the time Brian went back to P.E. class, he was smiling, at least for a while.

I think that, of all my students, Brian and Dustin tugged most at my heartstrings. Providentially, the two little guys had found kindred spirits in one another, both having come from broken homes and both loving to draw pictures better than just about anything in the world. During the following summer I tried to contact Brian but couldn't find him. I hoped he and his mother had moved somewhere to rejoin his dad. But I did locate Dustin, invited him to visit us at the lake, and on a sunny afternoon, I picked him up at his home. His grandmother told me he had gotten up four times during the night to see if it was time to go to my house. As I buckled him in the seat of my van, it was obvious he was ecstatic.

"Miz Freeman," he lisped, "I've had teachers before, but I *never* had one want to take me home!"

On the last day of school when I said goodbye to the children, I told them it had been a wonderful first year for me. (Now that it was over, I was already remembering the best times most.) Christopher of the big blue eyes and long lashes looked astonished.

"You mean this was your first year to teach school? *Man,* Mrs. Freeman, you learned a *lot!*" he declared.

Yes, Christopher, I learned a lot.

I learned that every child is special. I wish I could describe each one. Every one gifted and talented and treasured by their teacher. If any of my students gets to read this book, I want you to know Mrs. Freeman thinks of you and prays for you still. You will always be my first class, the smartest, sweetest group of seven-year-olds in the entire "Great State of Texas" to me.

I also learned that the people who teach our children are absolute heroes if they just keep showing up on Monday and are still on their feet by Friday. I am no longer naive about all that teachers do. I understand the sacrifices, as well as the rewards. So, hug a teacher today. He/she can use it.

Another hard but vital lesson I learned is to realize I have to say "no" at times to good things in order to keep my life in balance and my priorities straight. I loved my students, my amazingly patient principals, and my fellow teachers, but I love my own children and husband even more. And to be honest, I love myself enough to know I need time to be alone in order to be at peace with myself, my family, and my Savior. For me, I had to make a choice.

An excellent wife... smiles at the future...
she looketh well to the ways of her household.
PROVERBS 31:10, 26- 27, NASB
❧

The Nightcrawler Years

It was a shock to realize Zachary had turned thirteen during the winter. Ready or not, we were entering the teenage zone: the stage when an adolescent's brain synapses quit firing while the rest of their body races toward adulthood. I had the feeling I had not made the decision to become a full-time homemaker a month too soon.

More and more often I was finding myself in conflict with Zach over a topic I remember as a source of tension between Mother and David during his teen years. I had sworn I'd be smart enough and strong enough to avoid the conflict, but it was upon me. The topic is, of course, hair.

Picture this: bottom half of head is shaved to the scalp, top half is left to grow at will. He then parts the mop down the middle and lets it fall so that he comes out of the bathroom ready for school looking exactly like Alfalfa from the "Our Gang Comedies," circa 1936. The hair fountains from the part, in palm tree fashion, exactly as boys wore their hair during the Depression. He calls it "cool." I call it a bad hair day.

The topic of hair, however, fell into second place in order of importance recently when Zach lost his temper and took it out on his bedroom wall. This resulted in a dent in the wall and a five hundred dollar medical bill for a broken fist. The call went out. 1-800-MOTHER.

"Was it the knuckle bone directly below the little finger on the right hand?" she inquired.

"Well, yes. How did you know?"

"Because David broke the same bone when he was Zach's age. Only he broke his on someone else's chin. It's called the boxer's fracture. Welcome to the teenage zone, Honey."

"HELP!" was about all I could muster.

"Well, whatever you do, keep your sense of humor. Don't ever stop talking and hugging. Try to keep conflict over non-earth-shattering topics to a minimum. Discipline with less emotional turmoil than I did—but *do* discipline.

"You will blow it on occasion, but just remember, no matter how good a job you do raising the kids, you are still going to raise four little sinners in need of the grace of God."

I hung up the phone feeling somewhat better. I grabbed for pencil and paper. "Let's see now..." I licked the pencil and wrote, "(1) Keep sense of humor. (2) Discipline. (3) Keep huggin' and talkin.' (4) Even if we do it all perfectly, the kids won't turn out that way."

Just then the phone rang, and it was Mother again. "I forgot the most important thing: Pray a lot—with Scott—together. It will make all the difference."

I continued taking mental stock and decided the sense of humor thing shouldn't be all that hard, given my Erma Bombeck vow. I'd been working on that since they were toddlers. Besides, the kids were all developing their own senses of humor, and getting to be a lot of fun in the process.

One morning as we were about to leave the driveway for school, I realized I had forgotten to eat breakfast, so I asked Zachary to run get me a banana.

The next thing I knew he was running toward the house with his arms flattened against his ribs and his head cocked to one side. Then he turned around and ran back to the car in that same peculiar way—without a banana for my breakfast.

"Son! What are you doing?" I demanded. He looked back at me with sincere surprise.

"Didn't you tell me to run like a banana?"

At least Zachary and I were still hugging and talking. I was reminded of a great evening with the kids not long ago when we had watched a James Bond movie together. Bond had narrowly escaped death as he dropped miraculously from a plane onto a yacht in front of a beautiful woman. Then he cooly introduced himself. "Bond. James Bond."

Rachel was supposed to be cleaning her room instead of watching TV, so I tactfully reminded her of it.

"How's your room, Rachel?" I asked.

"Duhty," she answered, doing a perfect imitation of the famous secret agent. "Very duhty."

I laughed but dispatched her to her room while I, feeling a sudden rush of domesticity, dispatched myself to the kitchen to bake a pie. Not owning a pastry cutter, I resorted to cutting the shortening into the flour with two sharp knives. The flashing steel caught Zeke's eye.

"Ah-so," he observed, "Num Chuck Mom."

Zach hitched his stool up to the opposite side of the counter and offered his observation. "Nah," he said, "she's Mother Scissorhands."

Maybe humor *will* help carry us through this wormy stage, however corny it may get. I knew Mother had suffered all our teenage agonies as if they were her own, but I also knew beyond a shadow of a doubt she'd had a lot of laughs during those difficult years. She had kept a big brown envelope for each of us marked, "Becky's Treasures," "David's Treasures," and so forth. Sometimes when we get together, we drag out the envelopes. We usually end up rolling in the floor.

It's easy to track the changes in the notes we wrote to her as we neared, and then entered, the teen years. Rachel's notes are generally matter of fact and to the point. One of my favorites from her first grade year reads, "I love God and Mother." Another school paper reads, "Plants live in deart. Plants need to be waterd some. The end. roten by Rachel Arnold."

By the third grade, her notes became more sophisticated, even manipulative. One afternoon when Mother was out, Rachel took a telephone message. It read, "Momma, I have to go to the Dintest Jan. 10 - 1972. If you *Love me* you'll tell me to stay home."

As she neared junior high age, her notes changed slightly, "Mom, I've been borrowing pencils from my boyfriend cause I'm out. Don't buy me any."

During the school year, Mother felt we ought to eat a standard breakfast of eggs, bacon, toast and juice (this was before she learned about happy DL and lousy DL). I have never been much for breakfast anyway, but none of us liked eggs, and all of us had written notes to Mother about them at one time or another.

Rachel's got right to the point, "I hate eggs, I do!" while mine reflected a certain agony of the soul, "That was all I could eat—I got a stomach ache from them—but they tasted good—but don't give them to me again because I get a stomach ache. Anonomys"

David's egg notes had a man-of-the-world quality about them since they were written after he was in high school. At least three of them dealt with a situation which may reveal that my absent mindedness just might be inherited.

Mother had a tendency to put eggs on to boil and leave home for the day. David had a tendency to drop in from school to eat lunch at home and find the eggs exploded all over the kitchen, the pan dancing bright red on the burner. David would turn off the heat, set the pan in the sink to cool, and nonchalantly write notes like, "Good job, Mom!" or "Well, Mom, I hope you like your eggs hard!" and finally, "Well, Mom, you did it again!"

Both Mother and Daddy went through the phase when they felt we should have some musical training, especially since we all loved music. They thought we would take to lessons like a sick kitten to a warm brick. I made it through two years of piano lessons but refused to play when there was a single person in the house to hear it. Then came voice lessons, and in desperation, I penned another tactful note:

Dear Mother,

I do not like voice lessons. Here are the reasons: (1) I'm tired of quacking; (2) I have not got to sing words and even if I did, she wouldn't like it; (3) she said, 'Be careful, don't strain, I don't want to make your voice any worse than it is'; (4) I worry all week about it and I sweat."

Mother had already told me that she and Daddy agreed each of us had our hardest year in the eighth grade, which of course, became their hardest year with each of us.

"This is the year," she had warned, "when otherwise reasonably nice thirteen-year-olds become carnivorous. They will eat each other alive in their attempts to become part of the in crowd."

I knew why she felt that way. When I was thirteen, I don't know which I was more thankful for; the fact that Jesus saved me from hell or that He saved me from drowning in junior high peer pressure. Sometimes I think they may be one and the same.

On a weekend retreat with my youth group from church, I found the Lord through a simple prayer as I lay on my bunk looking at the stars through my cabin window. The next day I was sure it was my radiance that lit up the morning. Having found a friend in Jesus, I never felt loneliness again, even when on the outskirts of the in crowd.

Sometimes during eighth grade, I would take my Bible and read it in the school bathroom stall to avoid the cliques chattering away with each other in the cafeteria. It sounds pitiful, but it gave me strength and hope and before long, I had an increasing group of good friends I enjoyed all the way through high school.

Several of us began bringing our lunches to school and then at lunch break, we would walk to my house, where we rounded out the lunches or whipped up something for ourselves from the fridge. We giggled and laughed like all high school girls do, but we also shared our hearts and prayed together. We may even have offered a prayer of gratitude that we were not still in junior high. I'm sure Mother did. But then my little brother entered eighth grade purgatory.

One evening during David's eighth grade year, he was supposed to go back to school for rehearsal with a small, elite choral group for which he had been chosen. (Aside from the fact that he had a nice voice, he was the only boy in eighth grade whose voice had sufficiently changed that he could sing a baritone solo.) Mother and Daddy knew he was struggling with feeling shut out of the group, but felt he should be made to participate in the hope he would eventually feel that he belonged. They insisted he go, and he left the house angry and upset. By midnight, he had not returned.

Mother called every friend she knew to call, Daddy drove to every place he could think of that David might possibly be, and then they settled down in the darkened living room to wait for dawn and to pray. I crept from bed and sat up with them, wrapped in a quilt but still trembling as if I were having a chill.

When daylight came, Daddy and I started out again to look for David, first in the nearby woods. I'll never forget the sound of Daddy's voice calling for David, nor the drive to the police station to fill out a missing person's report.

We had already checked with all the hospitals in our area, but while Daddy and I were gone, Mother thought of one more friend of David's they hadn't particularly approved of, and she jumped in her car and drove to his house. She rang the doorbell several times before the sleepy headed boy slowly opened the door.

"Noel," she said, fighting back tears, "is David here?"

He nodded and left the door ajar, and soon David appeared, looking a little defiant, but sad and sheepish as well.

"Davey," Mother said softly, "let's go home." He nodded and they drove home in silence. Mother fixed him some breakfast, keeping an eye on the drive so she could let Daddy know immediately that David was safe. When we arrived, she hurried to meet us with the good news. Daddy ran inside, took David in his arms and his cries of relief echoed through the house.

All of us cried that morning, including David, and it was the last time he ever stayed out all night without permission. In his sophomore year in high school, we were discussing that Rachel was having a hard time in eighth grade, and he shocked us all by declaring, "Man, I *loved* junior high!"

One of several positive things that came out of that awful night was that Mother and Daddy began to set aside Friday evening, when we three kids were all usually out somewhere, to pray for us. They would build a fire in the fireplace and sit on the rug in front of it together and pray for us—for our safety, for our spiritual well-being and for our futures.

Not long after Zach hit the wall, Daddy told me about a visit he had just made to see David and Barb and Tyler in Indiana, where they live in a small bungalow situated on a river. Daddy, David, and Tyler spent the entire morning floating down the river in a boat. Little Tyler, age four, never once mentioned being tired or restless.

Daddy was amazed that David had taught his young son to cast from the boat already, and, somewhere around mid morning, Tyler landed a small fish. His enormous brown eyes danced and his dimpled face almost split open with his smile. As Daddy finished telling me about that morning, his eyes grew misty and his voice had a catch in it.

"I was very aware," he smiled, "that life had come full circle for me, and I had been given the great privilege of watching my son being a great dad to *his* son. Going through those hard teenage years seemed enormously worthwhile."

I'm sure Daddy meant to encourage me with the story. And sure 'nuff, he did.

Sons are a heritage from the Lord,
children a reward from him.

PSALM 127:3

Are You a Man
or a Worm?

From the desk where I type, our backyard is in full view, with the lake beyond. Almost the entire half acre is covered with items of metal, wood, or rubber, and Scott assures me every item will eventually become essential. When it does there it will be without cost, because he had the foresight to haul it home.

I have compiled the following inventory, to be sung to the tune of "A Partridge in a Pear Tree."

In our lakeside backyard my husband gave to me,
Twelve pipes a laying,
Eleven Schwinns a swarming,
Ten boards a warping,
Nine puppies barking,
Eight trash cans filling,

Seven cans a rusting,
Six bowls of dogfood,
Five Lawn Mo-wers!
Four fighting kids,
Three gas tanks,
Two buildings, outhouse style,
And a bass boat whose engine has expired!

Given the success of the television show, "Home Improvement," I feel confident I am not the only woman who has a husband in love with backyard junk and most of all, "man" tools.

Today's man is not satisfied with the old "hitting-the-thumb-with-the-hammer" accident. A man of the nineties can now shoot himself to death with a twopenny nail. Scott has observed a contractor securely shish-kabob his thumb to his forefinger while trying to nail a simple board to a simple wall. Ah, progress!

In fact, Scott very nearly lost the ability to father children as the result of an encounter with a "man saw." It happened when he casually walked up behind a buddy who happened to be wielding a circular saw. Seventeen stitches on his upper, inner thigh convinced him to never *casually* approach anyone with a power tool of any kind again. He even gets skittish when I plug in my electric handmixer.

Power hand tools excite almost any man, but real men almost always go on to bigger things. To really get *my* man salivating, it takes *heavy machinery.*

His first introduction to this addiction came with his first job after we were married, where he operated a forklift for a firm which produced medical supplies. It took him hardly any time at all to wedge the forklift between the ceiling above and the concrete floor beneath. He found himself and his machine sitting at a forty-five degree angle for some time. It began to seem like an eternity after the news buzzed over the intercom that the president of the company was touring the building and would be in his area shortly.

One summer while we were vacationing in Florida in a posh resort (thanks to sharing the rent with three families), Scott almost ran himself down with his own van. It was hard not to notice that our old Chevy van seemed a bit out of its league among the Cadillacs, Mercedes, and Jaguars, even before it began to make embarrassing noises. Scott felt compelled to play auto-mechanic-man in full view of all the well-to-do vacationers strolling about in their tennis whites.

In his attempt to repair the U-joints on the vehicle, he jacked the back wheels of the big, heavy, awkward machine onto a curb and crawled underneath. Apparently, it is important to put the emergency brake on when removing the U-joint of a car, because the "park" thing doesn't work once the U-joint is gone.

Scott remembered this when he found himself joyriding across the road, hanging on to the underside of the van for dear life. Thank the Lord, he escaped with only a few road burns on his backside, his macho image only slightly the worse for wear.

He loves man-sized machines, and he comes by it honestly. His father, Jim, rode a huge motorcycle to work for nearly thirty years. Now that Jim is retired, he spends his days in his garage, happily tinkering with his BMW between road rallies.

Scott's grandfather was also a motorcycle man, back in the days when motorcycles were called scooters. Bev, Scott's mom, thinks nothing of driving alone across the country to snow ski for a weekend, and his long, tall brother, Kent, drives a diesel truck with a gooseneck trailer even if he's only going to the local Get-It-Kwik for a loaf of bread. His sister, Laura, can outmaneuver most men driving a tractor, and in the company of her brothers can also blow gaskets, rotate distributors, and re-throttle spark plugs. (I'm pretty sure that's what I've heard them say.)

My side of the family is another matter entirely. I once purchased a Little Tikes™ picnic table in a box, and, in my attempt to assemble it, produced a flat plastic barge which the kids liked even better. Certainly, my father is not one who could be called even remotely handy. He refers to caulk, the builder's best friend, as "gookum pucky," and once managed to gash his head while operating a lawn sprinkler. After thirty-eight years of marriage, Mother keeps a phone number for a repairman whose ad reads, "We fix what your husband fixed." The only other man I know who might be Daddy's equal is our friend, Gary. When working alongside Gary, Scott truly appears to be a mechanical wizard.

Gary watched in awe as Scott miraculously fixed their broken dryer—by plugging it in. He became very nearly transfixed with wonder when Scott unclogged their overflowing commode by using—as a sheer stroke of plumbing genius—a plunger.

When we first met Gary and his wife, Mary, they had just moved to the country from Dallas and bought a lovely older home with acreage. The older couple from whom they bought the house were very sentimental about one particular young tree in the front yard.

"We planted it in memory of a dear relative," they explained reverently. "We'd appreciate it if you'd take good care of it."

Gary, eager to experience rural life to its fullest, purchased a new, bright red riding mower for his acreage. At last the day came for Gary to mount the mower. He thrilled as the engine roared to life, and he slipped it into gear, man and machine moving as one entity. Mary stepped out of their new home just in time to see him flatten the memorial sapling. Struggling to gain control, he backed over it again from the opposite direction. The lawn mower seemed to have a mind of its own.

The next evening, Gary courageously climbed on the mower again. This time Mary sat sipping coffee in the kitchen, a safe distance from Gary and his machine, watching him through the patio door. He seemed to be doing better than the day before. Suddenly, over the rim of her coffee cup, Mary saw headlights coming toward her.

"Surely not," Mary thought. Gary and the monster mower proceeded to hum steadily toward the patio door as she grabbed her coffee and backed up quickly from the table. The lawn mower collided with the door like some toothy creature out of a horror movie and proceeded to eat and digest the screen.

Mary takes no chances these days. When Gary is mowing, children and dogs are not allowed outside. She says he is the only man she knows who needs an air bag on his lawn mower.

On any given Saturday morning, Scott's neighborhood buddies appear from nowhere like June bugs to a back porch light, drawn by the roar of serious mechanical equipment in operation—be it chain saw or Weed Eater.™ Wally, a sweet grandfather of six, is the worst little boy of them all. He sometimes appears at the door asking to borrow a tool or a trailer, but I know he is actually hoping to find Scott fiddling around with some piece of machinery in the backyard. I've decided it's the "man" way of finding out if friends can "come out and play."

Before long, Scott peeks around the corner with his Saturday cup of coffee in hand and Wally by his side, with the eager look in his eyes that says, "Can I go, huh, can I, please, huh, can I?"

What's a wife to say to two grown up little boys? So, I put another pan under the dripping kitchen sink I had thought I might ask Scott to fix and give him the goahead.

During the spring after I had decided to turn in my resignation but while I was still teaching, I was jolted awake at 6:30 A.M. by an earthquake. Or so it seemed. I grabbed my robe and vibrated toward the source of the racket. There sat my husband atop a bulldozer (who knows where he got it?) digging a swimming pool-sized hole in our backyard (who knows why?). As far as I've been able to determine, he dug the hole purely for the fun of it, and thoroughly enjoyed filling it back up again the next day—for the same reason.

I watched Scott from the window as he toiled with the bulldozer in the sun, his muscles rippling with moisture. I felt a fresh surge of attraction for this man, realizing with affection that he looked good, even in sweat. With that flush of tenderness, I went to my leaky kitchen sink and filled a glass with water, then popped in a few ice cubes. I walked down the backdoor steps and waited for Scott to notice my presence and turn off the engine. When all was safe, I lifted the glass in his direction.

"Are we playing with our Tonka Toys™ this morning, sweetheart?" I asked coyly.

He pulled on the brake lever, reached gratefully for the water, wiped his moustache, and grinned. I noted the Tom Selleck lines on each side of his mischievous smile. Muscles, sweat, mischievous smiles—they always lower my resistance.

"Becky?" he said in his most endearing "little boy" voice.

"Yes, Scott?" I answered, trying to appear nonchalant about the huge crater in my yard.

"I like my tractor," he grinned.

This was news?

He released the brake and the engine roared again. Before my very eyes he transformed into a boy of about eight, eyes sparkling with adventure, and "vroomed" his big toy around the sandpile mountain. I couldn't help but enjoy watching him play "Big Guy" because he gets such a kick out of it. It's reassuring to know he can handle (and enjoy) tasks that would overwhelm me. Vital tasks, like, digging really big holes. I'm sure if he'd lived in an earlier time, he would have been a Dan'l Boone.

But in the twentieth century, my kitchen sink is dripping and I need to empty the bucket again. I wonder if it would work if I rented a jackhammer and told Scott he could chisel up the entire driveway in exchange for fixing the sink. Probably not. A leaky faucet is no—vroom, vroom, vroom—"man" job!

So God created man in his own image,
in the image of God he created him;
male and female he created them.
God saw all that he had made, and it was very good.
GENESIS 2:27, 31
&

___

Worm Sunny Days Back Home

Right now, I am pinching myself to remind me that this is not a dream. It is summertime and the livin' is easy. Fish are jumpin' all over the lake. I've been sleeping everyday until 10:00 A.M. My house is clean, I have seen that most glorious of sights, the bottom of the laundry basket! I may even become what is called "centered."

My husband, after a year-long diet of corn dogs and popsicles, almost broke down when I served him a hot meal with *three items* on his plate.

"And it's not on a stick!" he blubbered.

Best of all, I am enjoying real *communication* with my children—without yawning. We have even played badminton and gone swimming and whipped up a batch of burnt oatmeal cookies together.

Seriously though, we are in a rather scary place when we consider my not working and what the future holds, such as college tuition for four. I realize I may eventually have to go back to work, at least part-time. If so, I would much prefer to operate out of my home.

Maybe I could be a one woman show for ladies' clubs. I could write the invitations, cater the dinner, give a humorous talk, sing a song or two, maybe even learn to tap dance. Of course, all of this would probably be done with my dress on inside-out and backwards, wearing one red and one black shoe, my hair and forehead dyed plum purple, and an accidental eyebrow pencil mustache. Whatever it takes.

But Scott and I have learned some valuable lessons from my short-lived career. For one, our family is too precious and our time with our children is too short to let them become merely an "add on" to another busy life. Any possibility of outside work will have to allow me the time and energy to keep my family first, worms and all.

I once thought that when all my children were in school, the timing would be perfect for me to have a career outside the home. But I had forgotten how much it meant to me, as a child and as a teenager, to have my mother at home. She was nearly always available to talk, sometimes over cookies and milk and sometimes over dirty dishes if her day had been hectic, but she was *there*. And frankly, I needed her. And frankly, my kids need me right now more than most things money can buy.

As for college degrees, Scott and I managed to get ours by working, scholarships, grants, and government loans. Surely God can provide for our kids just as He provided for us. He's already done some pretty amazing providing, come to think about it.

The scariest thing is realizing Zach is only four years away from being ready for college—leaving home, maybe. Our children are growing up so fast. Lately I've been looking back over the years I had at home with them as preschoolers, and thinking of some of the precious memories I would have missed if I'd gone to college and to work sooner than I did.

"Mom? Look. I made a present for Jesus."

I look up from my reading to see Zachary, age four, holding a small box covered with a wash cloth. I gently lift the cloth and inspect the contents: a small Bible, some rocks, and his prized possession—a fishing lure. The living room grows quiet as the sun filters through the curtains, gilding Zachary's upturned and reverent face. We are standing, so it seems, on hallowed ground.

"I was wondering," he lisps, " does Jesus have a fishin' pole? I'll let Him borrow mine. And does He have a Bible already?" He pushes the box toward me. "Could you put this up high so I can give it to Him when we go to heaven?"

I remember the day Rachel spread her arms as wide as she could manage and exclaimed to her brothers, "God's pinkie is this big!" And the day she bounded to the car from Sunday School with the marvelous news that Jesus had straightened the "cricket" legs of a poor man in the Bible.

"But Mommy," she frowned, "I never saw a man that had bug legs before! Did he have to hop everywhere he went?"

As one might expect, Gabriel had his own burning question about God, asked, not once, but several times. It is that deeply debated theological question of the twentieth century: "Does God have hair in his nose?"

One day, when Gabe sat at the kitchen table happily making roll after roll of "rope" out of Play Doh™, he suddenly looked up as if to say, "Eureka!"

"Momma!" he excitedly blurted, "I figured out how God makes worms!"

Sometimes the task of teaching a child the difference be-tween God and a television super hero or Santa Claus provides another challenge for parents. During one period, I had been concentrating on explaining to Gabriel that God's power is real and that Superman's power is just pretend. I thought my lesson had been well taught and well received. A few days later, Gabe and I came upon a picture of Superman which offered a golden opportunity to check out what he had absorbed.

"We know who has the *real* power, right, little buddy?" I probed.

"Yep," he replied without a moment's hesitation. "Batman!"

As December approached, Gabriel gave me reason for believing there might still be hope for his theological education.

"Momma, I'm gonna ask God instead of Santa Claus for a metal detector," he announced, "cause He's the guy that can make a tree—right?"

By George, I think he's got it! Now for the lesson on "needs" versus "wants."

The incredible thing about childish, oft-distorted prayers is that so many times God will just right out *answer* them. Several years ago, when Zachary was about to turn five, I found him working like a Trojan, pulling weeds from our back yard. He told me God would give him a horse if he would just pull weeds every day. I explained that we only had a backyard the size of a horse's hoof and that God was proud of his work, but please don't expect a *real* horse. Maybe a toy horse. But of course, he would hear none of that. It would have to be a real horse.

To this day I shiver when I remember the afternoon, shortly before Zach's birthday, that a neighbor (who had no idea of Zach's prayer) called quite out of the blue.

"Would you possibly be interested in having a Shetland pony for the boys?" she asked. "We can keep it in our pasture if you could supply the hay."

Be assured, I asked Zach to pray for every conceivable need from then on. Come to think of it, I'd better get him started on his college education.

But one thing I do know. I fully expect one day to see Zachary, Ezekiel, Rachel Praise, and Gabriel, sitting near the feet of Jesus. They will be talking and laughing and perhaps casting for a celestial fish in the River of Life. Off to the side, surrounded by a heavenly glow may be a small yellowed box holding a tiny Bible and a few rocks—minus one fishing lure.

What more important work could I have done in my life than helping them make the choices to get them there?

But his mother treasured all these things in her heart.

LUKE 2:51

AFTERWORD

It is about 6:30 P.M. on a summer Friday evening, and I am sitting at my word processor in still-wet clothes, typing with very shaky hands and an unbelievably grateful heart. I want to get today's events down on paper before I forget them, although I can't imagine how they could possibly ever fade from my memory.

This week began like a lovely dream. As first-time authors, my mother and I suddenly found our manuscript being pursued by not one, but two wonderful Christian publishers at the same time. This, after two years of rejection slips and numerous re-writes, although we had had some close calls and significant encouragement along the way. I felt like an old maid who was suddenly presented with proposals of marriage from Tom Selleck *and* Tom Cruise—a delicious dilemma.

I had spent the day pinching myself to be sure it was real, not simply a euphoric, fog-like movie. As I ran errands about town (as if I were an ordinary mortal), I enjoyed imaginary conversations with the people I met while standing in line at various counters.

"Ahem," I mentally intruded upon several, "you may be unaware of this fact, but you probably should know you are standing in the presence of a soon-to-be-famous author."

Heady stuff. But that was an eternity ago. This afternoon, within five minutes, everything changed.

Happily sitting by the lake reading and lounging in the sun, I kept half an eye on half a dozen kids frolicking in the shallow water. A car pulled into the drive and my friend, Janet, stepped out with her son, fourteen-year-old Clint. She had come to pick up her daughter, Cricket, one of Rachel's best friends. I was delighted to see one of the few people I had not yet told about the book, and I immediately blurted out the morning's events, which had even included a *conference call* from one publisher.

I had in mind to jokingly say, "I'll have my people get in touch with your people and we'll 'do lunch.'" However, before I could offer this nifty line, Zachary verbalized one sentence that shot through me like a bullet, reducing me to complete and instantaneous panic.

"Mom," he said, half-worried, half-joking, "Is Gabe dead?"

"What?" I hollered.

"Well, he was swimming here a while ago. His friend, Jud, is out there in the deep water with a life jacket, but I don't see Gabe."

Sheer terror engulfed me when I saw Gabe's life jacket laying on the bank, telling its own story. He must have taken off his life jacket to practice swimming in the shallow water and (No, please God!) drifted into the deep.

A quick questioning of the seven people present revealed no one had seen him leave the water.

I immediately dived into the water, clothes and all, screaming irrationally to my child, who I had to assume for the moment was somewhere in that murky water. I groped around frantically for a minute or so, and every time I came to the surface, I begged Jud to remember when and where he had last seen Gabe.

"I don't remember," he insisted, "but I don't think Gabe is drownded."

Realizing we were getting nowhere, I ordered all present to form a human chain to comb the water where he had last been seen. Janet was an R.N.—she could perform CPR—if there was still time. Even as she began to untie her shoes, she had presence of mind to send her Clint to Jud's nearby house to check for Gabe and/or call 911. We moved forward, our eyes frantically scanning the water, now murkier than ever as we stirred up the sandy bottom.

In the next moment, the most wonderful sound I believe I've ever heard came from the top of the hill. Clint's adolescent voice rang out like a thousand heavenly angels to this mother's ear.

"He's up here!"

We all splashed to the bank, where my knees went out from under me, and I collapsed on the grassy shore.

"I think I might like to faint now," I managed. Little Jud stood over me with a water gun pointed in my direction, his expression a curious mixture of compassion and impatience.

"I *told* ya I didn't think he was drownded," he said flatly.

Gabe had been playing in Jud's backyard, without the faintest notion that anything unusual had been going on at the water's edge. I desperately wanted to run to my son and hug him to me, but my knees were still jelly. Finally, I found my pulse and trudged up the hill to Jud's house, my clothes dripping puddles around me. I found Gabriel fascinated with Jud's new puppy, and he waved me to come stroke the black bundle of fur. Walking past the pup, I went straight to Gabe, too weak to scold. I held him in my arms and absorbed him with my eyes. Then I held him and looked at him some more, and I thought what a marvelous child he was and how deeply I loved having his grimy little arms around my neck.

When the blood began to flow at a normal rate through my veins again, I reluctantly left Gabe to play with Jud as we had previously planned. I drove the short distance back to our cabin and found Scott outside mowing the lawn. He was blissfully unaware of all that had transpired. When he saw me, he stopped the mower and, anticipating the big news of the day to be from editors, walked toward me with open arms.

"Well," he beamed, "are we going to be published?"

"Yeah, yeah," I brushed aside his question and fell into his arms, the tears finally coming in a rush. "We're going to be published. But did you know we have the most precious five-year-old boy in the world? And he's *alive!*"

It is now 11:30 P.M., about four hours since I wrote that last sentence and I am now warm and dry. It's unusually quiet in the house, considering we have seven children sleeping here. This summer has been one continual come-and-go party. I never know which of my kids will grace us with their presence at breakfast. But here in the living room, with a dim light shining from over the kitchen sink, Gabriel lies serenely asleep on the couch. He is still in his cut-offs, with no shirt. One arm lies above his dark head in relaxed abandonment.

He had planned to spend the night with Jud, but Jud's mother brought him home a couple of hours after the drowning incident because he had developed a headache. When they arrived, Scott and I had elbowed each other all the way to the front door, each wanting to be the first to receive our son into our arms. Scott beat me to him, and to the aspirin bottle for his headache, and to the rocking chair to rock him, but we took turns kissing Gabe's cheeks and arguing over who loved him most. He fell asleep between us, loving all the attention. Scott laid him on the couch where I now watch him sleeping. Before going off to bed, Scott said in a teasing whisper, "Don't let him drown again. I like him."

I can still feel a physical ache around my heart at the memory of the afternoon down by our beloved lake—the agony of searching for Gabriel's body, knowing that seconds count, the look on his brothers' and sister's faces as they feared the worst for their little brother—and the sudden awareness of the incredible fragility of life.

I probably will never be angry with any of my children again. At least, not for several days. At the moment, I could eat each one of them with a spoon. (For the uninitiated, this is actually a term of endearment in the South.) Earlier, Janice called to check on me and to make sure I was up to having seven children spend the night.

"You bet!" I said without hesitation. "I just *love* children. I'm looking forward to having a houseful of them tonight."

Perspective. I had prayed this week that God would continually remind me of what is truly important. Throughout the week, the children have been locked out of my room for hours at a time while I had "important business" to conduct by phone. There were editors with whom I needed to negotiate, and thoughts about how to market the book (the book that tells parents how important it is to cherish time with their children). I had been generally spacey—out to lunch. At one point Gabe had lost all patience and pulled on the leg of my shorts.

"Have your feet come down to the ground yet?" he demanded jealously.

I picked up the phone for the fiftieth time that week, frowned and shook my head to quiet him. As he walked sulkily out the door, I heard him groan.

"I wish this wasn't a special day any more," he muttered.

It has been the best of days and the worst of days, a dickens of a day, so to speak; a wonderful book contract offer, combined with what seemed like a brush with the death of my child. I feel as if I have been on a roller coaster ride that left me more than a little woozy. I agree with Gabe. I am ready for this special day to be over.

Dear Lord,

Please don't put me through any more "drownding experiences." I *get* it. I really do. Without my husband and my children, worldly accomplishments would be meaningless. Thank You for Scott, Zach, Zeke, Rachel, and Gabriel.

As for being an author, I know You will keep me humble. That is a fairly easy job for You, as I usually take the fall before the pride goeth too far. And maybe this is the beginning of the provision for our family I have been praying for.

Use me as I strive to be honest about who I am: a flawed human being who is completely loved, accepted and forgiven by the King of kings, who somehow delights in calling Himself my friend. As my friend, You have tasted my tears. As my friend, You have shared and inspired my laughter.

May those who read this book come away blessed and refreshed and aware that no matter how messed up we are (and somehow everyone secretly seems to think they are more messed up than everyone else), You are absolutely wild about us. And You want me—us—to know joy even when life hands us a worm, or a bucket of them.

And by the way, in case I haven't mentioned it before, thank You. *Thank You* for Scott, Zach, Zeke, Rachel, and Gabriel. I am so glad they're all home tonight, safely tucked in bed. And that they are breathing nicely. (Okay, so I checked.) I'm still just a little nervous, that's all.

In Jesus' name, Amen.

Now unto him
who is able to do exceedingly abundantly
above all that we ask or think,
according to the power that worketh in us.

EPHESIANS 3:20, KJV